REVELATION:

DISPENSATIONALLY CONSIDERED

A GRACE EXPOSITIONAL COMMENTARY

Dr. David Alan Greene

GRACEWORD PUBLISHING

Contents

To Darlena, Matthew, and Karla

"The book of Revelation is less about the judgment of those who have rejected God's salvation and more about the culmination of God's restoration of Creation and the revelation of His Son."

x

Acknowledgements

Revelation: Dispensationally Considered is the last commentary in the New Testament to be publishing. Like the others, it is part of the series called *A Grace Expositional Commentary*. While working on these books, either as editor or author, I am surrounded by people who continue in their encouragement. My mother Frances Greene has lived with me since becoming a widow. She has read all the books published by GraceWord Publishing, LLC. Her views and encouragement along with those of Jon and Sharon McMahon have spirited me on to complete the task. In like-mindedness, these folks are eager to share and encourage other believers to become strong in the faith. Thank you to those who continually seek to learn, understand, and enjoy the Bible rightly divided.

Introduction

For those readers who have decided, like some do, to go to the end of a novel to find out the who-dunit, you are going to be disappointed. The purpose of this book is much like the law. If you break the law, then there are consequences. You should know the law in advance. If you speed, then you will get a speeding ticket. If you get enough of them, then you can lose your license. Throughout the Bible, God has continually made it clear that there are consequences of sin. He has presented two means of salvation. The first is the Gospel of the Kingdom. This is the gospel preached by Christ when He came to earth to confirm the promises made to the fathers. (See Romans 15:8.) The other is the Gospel of Grace. This other gospel was given to the Apostle Paul. It is offered to all individuals, both Jew and Gentile, to be saved by God's grace through faith. By the time we get to the Tribulation, those who were saved by the Gospel of Grace have been removed at the Rapture. Therefore, those who remain, both Jew and Gentile, must face the events described in Revelation.

Before we begin, it is important that you know this book is not an introductory book. When writing syllabi for seminary courses, some courses have prerequisite courses. Students must have a foundational knowledge before they can take that class. Education is like building something. There must always be a foundation before a building can be built. Therefore, I recommend two of my books. They provide surveys of the entire Bible and show how it is held together cohesively. The first is *Letters To Theophilus: Are You Ready For The End Times?* This book presents the Bible from the perspective of a Gentile or non-Jew. It presents the Gospel of Grace which is offered to Gentiles and Jews individually. I like to say that the other book is the "other side of the same coin." It is called *The Glorious Destiny of Israel: The Fulfillment of G-d's Promises and Prophecies to Israel.* This book applies specifically to the children of Abraham. It is to this latter group that the Apostle John wrote the book of Revelation.

In *The Glorious Destiny*, we look at Daniel's timeline which brings the Bible to its conclusion. At the end of this timeline, God establishes the everlasting Kingdom promised to King David. In the book of Revelation, this eternal King Who will sit upon

David's throne is revealed. All that God has promised to Israel will be fulfilled. In the final days of Jesus' earthly ministry, the disciples were alone with Him. In the Gospel of Matthew, we read "And as he sat upon the mount of Olives, the disciples came unto him privately, saying, Tell us, when shall these things be? and what shall be the sign of thy coming, and of the end of the world?" (Matt. 24:3). Those who believe the Gospel of the Kingdom must have faith and keep their faith until the end. Those that do, will receive their salvation upon His return. Jesus validates Daniel's prophecy. Matthew 24:13-15:

> 13 **But he that shall endure unto the end, the same shall be saved. 14 And this gospel of the kingdom shall be preached in all the world for a witness unto all nations; and then shall the end come. 15 When ye therefore shall see the abomination of desolation, spoken of by Daniel the prophet, stand in the holy place, (whoso readeth, let him understand:)**

The prophecy foretells of the arrival of the Antichrist who is explained in greater detail in Revelation.

The Apostle John was the youngest of the Twelve. He had a close bond with Jesus similar to that of an older and younger brother. It is generally believed that John lived a long life unlike the other apostles. It was to him that this Revelation was given. John records his visions. As we read through this book, we will see the connection to the prophecies given to Israel. Most people are familiar with the seven-year tribulation. This comes from a prophecy found in Daniel 9. It concerns the arrival of the promised Kingdom, but to get to that point, there must be judgment. So severe is this judgment, that we are told that had it not been cut short no one would have survived. Matthew 24:21-22:

> 21 **For then shall be great tribulation, such as was not since the beginning of the world to this time, no, nor ever shall be. 22 And except those days should be shortened, there should no flesh be saved: but for the elect's sake those days shall be shortened.**

Those who are saved by grace through faith according to the Gospel of Grace have nothing to fear. Having received the righteousness of Christ, their salvation is secured by the holy Spirit of Promise. Their bodily redemption is guaranteed. (See Ephesians 1:13-14.)

When we read Revelation, we see that those who rejected God's salvation will be judged by the

Righteous One, Jesus Christ. The Tribulation is the period of time that is outlined in Revelation. Its purpose, like the refiner's fire, is to test the faith of true Israel. Do they believe that Jesus is their Messiah and the Son of God. Do they have faith in God's Word and faithfully follow His commandments. Again, He stated, "But he that shall endure unto the end, the same shall be saved" (Matt. 24:13). Keeping the Law is important for Israel. John 14:21:

> 21 He that hath my commandments, and keepeth them, he it is that loveth me: and he that loveth me shall be loved of my Father, and I will love him, and will manifest [reveal] myself to him.

Look at the verses that are often called The Great Commission. At His Ascension, Jesus instructs His Eleven Apostles to teach those who follow the Gospel of the Kingdom. Matthew 28:20:

> 20 Teaching them to observe all things whatsoever I have commanded you: and, lo, I am with you alway, even unto the end of the world. Amen.

We see in Genesis that there were two distinct groups. First, there was the nations which were created at the Tower of Babel. From out of this group

God called one person, Abram. This created the second group. At the Rapture, a third group, those saved by the Gospel of Grace, will be removed. Only the Gentile nations and Israel will remain at the time of the Tribulation. How God will deal with these two groups is foretold in Genesis 12:2-3:

> 2 **And I will make of thee [Abram] a great nation, and I will bless thee, and make thy name great; and thou shalt be a blessing:** 3 **And <u>I will bless them that bless thee, and curse him that curseth thee</u>: and in thee shall all families of the earth be blessed.**

This promise to bless and curse those who do so to the children of Abraham will be applied to the Gentiles at the end of the seven years. For those Gentiles who are not removed at the Rapture, the only choice for them is to bless Israel and suffer the wrath of the Antichrist.

1

Revelations 1

As we begin, we need to understand the meaning of the word *revelation*. The word comes from the Latin *revelatus* which means *to make known something or someone who was previously unknown or hidden*. Many people have heard of Jesus Christ, but few fully understand Who He is. Revelation 1:1:

> 1 **The Revelation of Jesus Christ, which God gave unto him, to shew unto his servants things which must shortly come to pass; and he sent and signified it by his angel unto his servant John:**

In the four gospels, it appears that the end times were imminent. The harvest of believers was "at hand" during the end of Christ's earthly ministry. Following His baptism by John the Baptist, He was led out into the Wilderness to be tested. When He returned He began His ministry, ". . . saying, The time is fulfilled, and the kingdom of God is at hand: repent ye, and believe the gospel" (Mark 1:15). The kingdom was indeed imminent, but it was temporarily suspended at its rejection. God made a final offer through Stephen who was subsequently stoned. (See Acts 6 and 7.) At Stephen's stoning, we are introduced to Saul who would become the Apostle to the Gentiles. Later, the book of Acts closes with a proclamation. Acts 28:25-29:

> **25 And when they [the Jews] agreed not among themselves, they departed, after that Paul had spoken one word, Well spake the Holy Ghost by Esaias the prophet unto our fathers, 26 Saying, Go unto this people, and say, Hearing ye shall hear, and shall not understand; and seeing ye shall see, and not perceive: 27 For the heart of this people is waxed gross, and their ears are dull of hearing, and their eyes have they closed; lest they should see with their eyes, and hear with their ears, and understand with their heart, and should be converted, and I should heal them. 28 <u>Be it known therefore unto you, that the salvation of God is sent unto the Gentiles, and that they will hear it.</u> 29 And when he had said these words, the Jews**

departed, and had great reasoning among themselves.

Paul, in writing to those saved by grace through faith in Rome, explains Israel's current state and God's purpose for this temporary delay. Romans 11:9-12:

> 9 **And David saith, Let their table be made a snare, and a trap, and a stumblingblock, and a recompence unto them:** 10 **Let their eyes be darkened, that they may not see, and bow down their back alway.**

> 11 **I say then, Have they [Israel] stumbled that they should fall? God forbid: but rather <u>through their fall salvation is come unto the Gentiles, for to provoke them to jealousy</u>.** 12 **Now if the fall of them be the riches of the world, and the diminishing of them the riches of the Gentiles; <u>how much more their fulness</u>?**

This hints of the coming glory promised to Israel, if they have faith, keep the commandments, and endure unto the end.

As a Jew, the Apostle John has been entrusted by God to record this revelation. It assures the blessings that true Israel will receive, again, if they continue in their faith and keep His commandments. Revelation 1:2-3:

> 2 **Who bare record of the word of God, and of the testimony of Jesus Christ, and of all things that he saw.** 3 **Blessed is he that readeth, and they that hear the words of this prophecy, and keep those things which are written therein: for the time is at hand.**

At the time John wrote this, he still believed that the time was "at hand." Its prophecy records the events that will unfold during the last seven years.

Like the four gospels and the eight Hebrew epistles preceding Revelation, this prophecy is written to Israel. It discloses their future and the coming King according to the Gospel of the Kingdom. Verses 4-6:

> 4 **[From] John to the seven churches which are in Asia: Grace be unto you, and peace, from him which is, and which was, and which is to come; and from the seven Spirits which are before his throne;**

As we go forward, we will see more references to the seven spirits. The number seven denotes perfection and may refer to the facets or attributes of the Holy Spirit found in Isaiah 11:2:

> 2 And <u>the spirit of the LORD</u> shall rest upon him, <u>the spirit of wisdom</u> and [the spirit of] <u>understanding</u>, <u>the spirit of counsel</u> and [the spirit of] <u>might</u>, the spirit of <u>knowledge</u> and [the spirit of] <u>the fear of the LORD;</u>

These seven spirits are before the throne of God and His Son to Whom God said, "Sit thou at my right hand, until I make thine enemies thy footstool" (Ps. 110:1).

In the Gospel of John, the apostle makes it clear that Jesus Christ has coexisted with God since before Creation. John 1:1-3:

> 1 In the beginning was the Word, and the Word was with God, and the Word was God. 2 <u>The same was in the beginning with God.</u> 3 All things were made by him; and without him was not any thing made that was made.

Therefore, Jesus has been a witness from the beginning. Verse 5:

> 5 **And from Jesus Christ, who is the faithful witness, and the first begotten of the dead . . ., and the prince of the kings of the earth . . . Unto him that loved us, and washed us from our sins in his own blood,**

Jesus Christ was the first to be resurrected from the dead by God. Therefore, He is referred to as "the first begotten" from the dead. In the future, their Messiah will be ruler over all the kings of the earth. John acknowledges His sacrifice through the shedding of His blood. Consistent with Israel's sacrificial system, Jesus Christ is both their Messiah and their Passover Lamb. John also recorded the words of John the Baptist, "Behold the Lamb of God, which taketh away the sin of the world" (Jn. 1:29).

God had Moses inform the children of Israel of His special purpose for them. Exodus 19:5-6:

> 5 **Now therefore, if ye will obey my voice indeed, and keep my covenant, then ye shall be <u>a peculiar treasure unto me above all people</u>: for all the earth is mine: 6 And <u>ye shall be unto me a kingdom of priests, and an holy nation.</u>**

These are the words which thou shalt speak unto <u>the children of Israel</u>.

They are to be "an holy nation." Here, the word *holy* means *to be separated unto God.* Revelation 1:6:

6 <u>**And hath made us kings and priests**</u> **unto God and his Father; to him be glory and dominion for ever and ever. Amen.**

John makes a reference to the circumstances of His Coming. We must not confuse this with His Appearing. To make an impression with a men's Bible Study, I said boots in the air and boots on the ground. As of the writing of this commentary, His Appearing is imminent. So, the Rapture can happen at any time. However, the former, His Coming, can only occur at the end of the seven-year Tribulation. John provides some facts about this event. Verse 7:

7 **Behold, he cometh with clouds; and every eye shall see him, and they also which pierced him: and all kindreds of the earth shall wail because of him. Even so, Amen.**

The event of His Coming will not be hidden. Everyone will see it. However, at that point in time, there will be great anguish. I believe this applies to those who injured Christ physically at His Crucifixion, but also those who continue to reject Him. Through His Apostle John, Christ makes the following bold statement of truth. Verse 8:

> 8 **I am Alpha and Omega, the beginning and the ending, saith the Lord, which is, and which was, and which is to come, the Almighty.**

Like the other Hebrew epistles, Revelation is written to Israel. James wrote, "to the twelve tribes which are scattered abroad" (Jas. 1:1). They are written to the faithful Jews who are waiting for the fulfillment of God's promises and prophecies. This does not mean that the non-Jews cannot benefit from them, but they are intended for the faithful Jews. John is one of the Twelve. He too is a fellow believer like the others who have faith in God's Word and await its fulfillment. Verse 9:

> 9 **I John, who also am your brother, and companion in tribulation, and in the kingdom and patience of Jesus Christ, was in the isle that is called Patmos, for the word of God, and for the testimony of Jesus Christ.**

The Isle of Patmos is located in the Aegean Sea which is not far from present-day Turkey. It was there that John received this revelation.

He continues. Verses 10-11:

10 I was in the Spirit on the Lord's day, and heard behind me a great voice, as of a trumpet, 11 Saying, I am Alpha and Omega, the first and the last: and, What thou seest, write in a book, and send it unto the seven churches which are in Asia; unto Ephesus, and unto Smyrna, and unto Pergamos, and unto Thyatira, and unto Sardis, and unto Philadelphia, and unto Laodicea.

John is to write down what he sees and send it to the seven churches listed above. The word *church* means *the called-out ones*. This information does not apply to those saved by the Gospel of Grace. However, it does apply to those saved by the Gospel of the Kingdom. They are waiting for the Coming of their King. It is about this King that John writes, "Behold, he cometh with clouds; and every eye shall see him" (v. 7).

John explains how he received this revelation from the Lord Himself. Verses 12-16:

12 And I turned to see the voice that spake with me. And being turned, I saw seven golden candlesticks; 13 And in the midst of the seven candlesticks one like unto the Son of man, clothed with a garment down to the foot, and girt about the paps with a golden girdle.

14 His head and his hairs were white like wool, as white as snow; and his eyes were as a flame of fire; 15 And his feet like unto fine brass, as if they burned in a furnace; and his voice as the sound of many waters. 16 And he had in his right hand seven stars: and out of his mouth went a sharp two-edged sword: and his countenance was as the sun shineth in his strength.

This is similar to the description of God Who placed Moses within a cleft of the rock. Notice that Moses could not see His face, but the Apostle John saw His eyes. Exodus 33:20-23:

20 And he said, Thou canst not see my face: for there shall no man see me, and live. 21 And the LORD said, Behold, there is a place by me, and thou shalt stand upon a rock: 22 And it shall come

to pass, while my glory passeth by, that I will put thee in a clift of the rock, and will cover thee with my hand while I pass by: 23 And I will take away mine hand, and thou shalt see my back parts: but my face shall not be seen.

The Apostle, clearly moved, fell at His feet as if he were dead. From the text, we can identify the One speaking as Jesus Christ, the Alpha and Omega. Verse 17-18:

17 And when I saw him, I fell at his feet as dead. And he laid his right hand upon me, saying unto me, Fear not; I am the first and the last: 18 I am he that liveth, and was dead; and, behold, I am alive for evermore, Amen; and have the keys of hell and of death.

The One standing before him is the One Who was crucified, dead, and buried. God raised Him from the grave and now He lives forevermore.

It is from the Risen Lord that John is receiving these instructions concerning what will soon be revealed to him. The number seven represents perfection and is used repeatedly. Verses 19-20:

19 Write the things which thou hast seen, and the things which are, and the things which shall be hereafter; 20 The mystery of the seven stars which thou sawest in my right hand, and the seven golden candlesticks. The seven stars are the angels of the seven churches: and the seven candlesticks which thou sawest are the seven churches.

2

Revelation 2

In his letter to Timothy, the Apostle Paul refers to "the Lord Jesus Christ, who shall judge the quick and the dead at his appearing and his kingdom" (2 Tim. 4:1). He is specifically speaking about the events we are now studying. Only Jesus Christ is righteous enough to judge. Please remember that the churches mentioned here are not believers of the Gospel of Grace. They were removed at the Rapture.

The following seven churches are groups who are saved by the Gospel of the Kingdom. Revelations 2:1-3:

> **1 Unto the angel of the church of Ephesus write; These things saith he that holdeth the seven stars in his right hand, who walketh in the midst of the seven golden candlesticks; 2 I know thy**

works, and thy labour, and thy patience, and how thou canst not bear them which are evil: and thou hast tried them which say they are apostles, and are not, and hast found them liars: 3 And hast borne, and hast patience, and for my name's sake hast laboured, and hast not fainted.

In spite of the good works of the church of Ephesus, they have fallen short in their faith. Christ reprimands them and urges them to repent. He wants them to return to their first love. Verses 4-6:

4 Nevertheless I have somewhat against thee, because thou hast left thy first love. 5 Remember therefore from whence thou art fallen, and repent, and do the first works; or else I will come unto thee quickly, and will remove thy candlestick out of his place, except [unless] thou repent. 6 But this thou hast, that thou hatest the deeds of the Nicolaitans, which I also hate.

Christ speaks to all who follow the Kingdom Gospel. This is a reoccurring theme. "But he that shall endure unto the end, the same shall be saved" (Matt. 24:13). If they overcome and endure to the end, then they will receive eternal life. Salvation is always a gift of God. However, based upon Israel's history of losing faith, true Israel must continue to demonstrate their faith by persevering unto the end. Verse 7:

> 7 **He that hath an ear, let him hear what the Spirit saith unto the churches; To him that overcometh will I give to eat of the tree of life, which is in the midst of the paradise of God.**

This is a confirmation of everything that Christ taught on earth. It was later taught by the Kingdom Apostles in the Hebrew epistles. Now, it is repeated here.

He continues with His message to the Kingdom Believers at Smyrna. Verses 8-10:

> 8 **And unto the angel of the church in Smyrna write; These things saith the first and the last, which was dead, and is alive; 9 I know thy works, and tribulation, and poverty, (but thou art rich) and I know the blasphemy of them which say they are Jews, and are not, but are the synagogue of Satan.**

Did you notice that He is aware of those who "say they are Jews, and are not, but are the synagogue of Satan" (v. 9). We know that He is addressing Jews specifically as the entire seven-year Tribulation concerns them. Jeremiah 30:7:

> 7 **Alas! for that day is great, so that none is like it: it is even <u>the time of Jacob's trouble</u>; but he shall be saved out of it.**

The last book in the Old Testament is Malachi. This Hebrew prophet wrote the following about the last days. In order to restore Creation, God must test to determine true Israel. Malachi 3:2-4

> 2 **But who may abide the day of his coming? and who shall stand when he appeareth? for he is like a refiner's fire, and like fullers' soap: 3 And he shall sit as a refiner and purifier of silver: and he shall purify the sons of Levi, and purge them as gold and silver, that they may offer unto the LORD an offering in righteousness.**
>
> 4 **Then shall the offering of Judah and Jerusalem be pleasant unto the LORD, as in the days of old, and as in former years.**

Through the trials and tribulations, they are to remain faithful unto death. If they do, then they will receive their reward: salvation along with "a crown of life." Verses 10-11:

> 10 **Fear none of those things which thou shalt suffer: behold, the devil shall cast some of you into prison, that ye may be tried; and ye shall have tribulation ten days: <u>be thou faithful unto death, and I will give thee a crown of life.</u>**
>
> 11 **He that hath an ear, let him hear what the Spirit saith unto the churches; <u>He that overcometh shall not be hurt of the second death.</u>**

The second death is permanent and from which there is no redemption. It is synonymous with the lake of fire and eternal separation from God.

John moves on to the third of the seven churches. Verses 12-13:

> 12 **And to the angel of the church in Pergamos write; These things saith he which hath the sharp sword with two edges; 13 I know thy works, and where thou dwellest, even where Satan's seat**

is: and thou holdest fast my name, and hast not denied my faith, even in those days wherein Antipas was my faithful martyr, who was slain among you, where Satan dwelleth.

He begins by commending the church, then he brings their short-falls to their attention. Again, He is speaking to the children of Israel! Verses 14-16:

14 But I have a few things against thee, because thou hast there them that hold the doctrine of Balaam, who taught Balac to cast a stumblingblock before the children of Israel, to eat things sacrificed unto idols, and to commit fornication. 15 So hast thou also them that hold the doctrine of the Nicolaitans, which thing I hate. 16 Repent; or else I will come unto thee quickly, and will fight against them with the sword of my mouth.

He is calling them to repentance which means a turning away from their activities. If they do not, then He will use the Word of God to judge them which He calls "the sword of my mouth."

Christ makes a general call to the churches for

them to overcome. For those Jews who do, they will receive a new name that only they will know. Verse 17:

> 17 **He that hath an ear, let him hear what the Spirit saith unto the churches; To him that overcometh will I give to eat of the hidden manna, and will give him a white stone, and in the stone a new name written, which no man knoweth saving [except] he that receiveth it.**

The church in Thyatira is the fourth of the seven churches. Verses 18-19:

> 18 **And unto the angel of the church in Thyatira write; These things saith the Son of God, who hath his eyes like unto a flame of fire, and his feet are like fine brass; 19 I know thy works, and charity, and service, and faith, and thy patience, and thy works; and the last to be more than the first.**

He knows their faith, patience, and their works. However, they have fallen short. By now, you should be convinced that Revelation cannot be written to those saved by grace through faith. Why? Upon believing, they received the righteousness of Christ.

Verses 20-28:

20 Notwithstanding I have a few things against thee, because thou sufferest [allow] that woman Jezebel, which calleth herself a prophetess, to teach and to seduce my servants to commit fornication, and to eat things sacrificed unto idols. 21 And I gave her space to repent of her fornication; and she repented not. 22 Behold, I will cast her into a bed, and them that commit adultery with her into great tribulation, except they repent of their deeds. 23 And I will kill her children with death; and all the churches shall know that I am he which searcheth the reins and hearts: and I will give unto every one of you according to your works.

24 But unto you I say, and unto the rest in Thyatira, as many as have not this doctrine, and which have not known the depths of Satan, as they speak; I will put upon you none other burden. 25 But that which ye have already hold fast till I come. 26 And he that overcometh, and keepeth my works unto the end, to him will I give power over the nations:

27 And he shall rule them with a rod of iron; as the vessels of a potter shall they be broken to shivers: even as I received of my Father. **28** And I will give him the morning star.

The following verse is the fourth time that John wrote these words. It will continue to be a significant reminder in the next chapter as well where he will repeat it three more times. Repetition in God's Word should be heeded. We will see that John places similar verses throughout Revelation 3. Let us say he is "hammering home" to the reader the importance of hearing what is being said. Verse 29:

29 He that hath an ear, let him hear what the Spirit saith unto the churches.

3

Revelation 3

As we begin, remember the importance of hearing what is being said. Similar to the previous three churches, John records the words spoken about the other three. Revelation 3:1-5:

> 1 **And unto the angel of the church in Sardis write; These things saith he that hath the seven Spirits of God, and the seven stars; I know thy works, that thou hast a name that thou livest, and art dead.** 2 **Be watchful, and strengthen the things which remain, that are ready to die: for I have not found thy works perfect before God.** 3 **Remember therefore how thou hast received and heard, and hold fast, and repent. If therefore thou shalt not watch, I will come on thee as a thief, and thou shalt not know what**

hour I will come upon thee. 4 Thou hast a few names even in Sardis which have not defiled their garments; and they shall walk with me in white: for they are worthy. 5 <u>He that overcometh, the same shall be clothed in white raiment; and I will not blot out his name out of the book of life, but I will confess his name before my Father, and before his angels.</u>

Much of the above content can be found in the four gospels. Nothing has changed. The Gospel of the Kingdom taught by Jesus Christ and preached by His apostles will be the same gospel preached in the latter-days. The Gospel of Grace is no longer available. God's offer or salvation by grace through faith alone has been withdrawn. Following the Rapture, only the Gospel of the Kingdom prevails. John wrote, "For whatsoever is born of God overcometh the world: and this is the victory that overcometh the world, even [that is to say] our faith" (1 Jn. 5:4). During this time of Jacob's testing, true Israel must keep their faith in the Word of God. Matthew 10:32-33:

32 Whosoever therefore shall confess me before men, him will I confess also before my Father which is in heaven. 33 But whosoever shall deny me before

men, him will I also deny before my Father which is in heaven.

Before John moves onto the next church, he repeats the words of warning. Verse 6:

6 He that hath an ear, let him hear what the Spirit saith unto the churches.

We come to the sixth of the seven churches called Philadelphia. Verses 7-12:

7 And to the angel of the church in Philadelphia write; These things saith he that is holy, he that is true, he that hath the key of David, he that openeth, and no man shutteth; and shutteth, and no man openeth; 8 I know thy works: behold, I have set before thee an open door, and no man can shut it: for thou hast a little strength, and hast kept my word, and hast not denied my name. 9 Behold, I will make them of the synagogue of Satan, which say they are Jews, and are not, but do lie; behold, I will make them to come and worship before thy feet, and to know that I have loved thee. 10 Because thou hast kept the word of my patience, I also will keep thee

from the hour of temptation, which shall come upon all the world, to try them that dwell upon the earth. 11 Behold, I come quickly: hold that fast which thou hast, that no man take thy crown.

12 Him that overcometh will I make a pillar in the temple of my God, and he shall go no more out: and I will write upon him the name of my God, and the name of the city of my God, which is new Jerusalem, which cometh down out of heaven from my God: and I will write upon him my new name.

For those who overcome evil when they are tested and hold fast to their faith, God will reward them. He assures them of this. Verse 13:

13 He that hath an ear, let him hear what the Spirit saith unto the churches.

The last of the seven churches is Laodicea. It is known as the "lukewarm" church because it is neither hot nor cold. Verses 14-21:

14 And unto the angel of the church of the Laodiceans write; These things saith

the Amen, the faithful and true witness, the beginning of the creation of God; 15 I know thy works, that thou art neither cold nor hot: I would [wish] thou wert cold or hot. 16 So then because thou art lukewarm, and neither cold nor hot, I will spue thee out of my mouth. 17 Because thou sayest, I am rich, and increased with goods, and have need of nothing; and knowest not that thou art wretched, and miserable, and poor, and blind, and naked: 18 I counsel thee to buy of me gold tried in the fire, that thou mayest be rich; and white raiment, that thou mayest be clothed, and that the shame of thy nakedness do not appear; and anoint thine eyes with eyesalve, that thou mayest see.

19 As many as I love, I rebuke and chasten: be zealous therefore, and repent. 20 Behold, I stand at the door, and knock: if any man hear my voice, and open the door, I will come in to him, and will sup with him, and he with me. 21 <u>To him that overcometh will I grant to sit with me in my throne, even as I also overcame, and am set down with my Father in his throne.</u>

Christ makes a promise to those who overcome the testing or tribulation, they will sit with Him upon His throne. He closes with the same assurance to those who listen.

> **22 He that hath an ear, let him hear what the Spirit saith unto the churches.**

In Revelation 2 and 3, John has received messages from God to the seven churches. To whom is he to deliver these messages? The word "church" simply means "the called-out ones." Here, it applies specifically to the Jews who are "called-out" by believing the Gospel of the Kingdom. These various "churches" have not been "measuring up" to the Lord's expectations. He praises them for their works, but then states that they are falling short. They are not demonstrating their worthiness to receive salvation at the Lord's Second Coming. When we understand this, we know that these messages to the seven churches cannot be for those who are saved by the Gospel of Grace. The content of this book applies to the time following the Rapture. Therefore, it can only be applied to the "churches" who follow the Gospel of the Kingdom.

4

Revelation 4

In Revelation, the Apostle John records voices he heard and the visions he saw from the Lord. Yet, John is not alone. The Apostle Paul had something similar happen to him. These are Paul's words in which he describes his own experience in the third person. 2 Corinthians 12:1-4:

> 1 **It is not expedient for me doubtless to glory. I will come to visions and revelations of the Lord.** 2 **I knew a man in Christ above fourteen years ago, (whether in the body, I cannot tell; or whether out of the body, I cannot tell: God knoweth;) such an one caught up to the third heaven.** 3 **And I knew such a man, (whether in the body, or out of the body, I cannot tell: God knoweth;)** 4 **How that he was caught up into para-**

dise, and heard unspeakable words, which it is not lawful for a man to utter.

This helps us to understand that John's experience for the Jews is not unlike Paul's experience for the Gentiles.

Revelation may seem like a challenge because it uses symbols. This is typical for prophetic allegory. We will not get bogged down with the symbolism. Instead, we will focus on the meaning of John's message. Revelation 4:1:

> 1 **After this I looked, and, behold, a door was opened in heaven: and the first voice which I heard was as it were of a trumpet talking with me; which said, Come up hither, and I will shew thee things which must be hereafter.**

Did the trumpet actually speak or did a herald blow the trumpet and, when John turned his attention to it, the herald spoke? We must stay focused on the message.

He writes about a throne in heaven with Someone sitting upon it. Verses 2-3:

> 2 **And immediately I was in the spirit:**

**and, behold, <u>a throne was set in heaven,
and one sat on the throne</u>. 3 And he that
sat was to look upon like a jasper and a
sardine stone: and there was a rainbow
round about the throne, in sight like
unto an emerald.**

Seeing the One Who is seated upon the throne, John
is constrained to use words alone to describe the glorious appearance of this Being. Through John, we are
receiving a glimpse of all the glory he beheld. He describes the surroundings. Verses 4-5:

**4 And round about the throne were four
and twenty seats: and upon the seats I
saw four and twenty elders sitting,
clothed in white raiment; and they had
on their heads crowns of gold. 5 And out
of the throne proceeded lightnings and
thunderings and voices: and there were
seven lamps of fire burning before the
throne, which are the seven Spirits of
God.**

John has been transported to heaven, but it is in the
future. Notice that the throne is surrounded by
twenty-four elders. In the Gospel of Matthew, Peter
asks Jesus what will the Twelve receive since they
gave up their earthly possessions. Here is His reply.

"And Jesus said unto them, Verily I say unto you, That ye which have followed me, in [when it comes to] the regeneration when the Son of man shall sit in the throne of his glory, ye also shall sit upon twelve thrones, judging the twelve tribes of Israel" (Matt. 19:28). Notice that Jesus stated that they will judge the children of Israel who are the twelve tribes.

John describes the surroundings of the throne creating a panorama for his readers. He does his best with words which are inadequate to describe this scene. Verses 6-8:

> 6 **And before the throne there was a sea of glass like unto crystal: and in the midst of the throne, and round about the throne, were four beasts full of eyes before and behind. 7 And the first beast was like a lion, and the second beast like a calf, and the third beast had a face as a man, and the fourth beast was like a flying eagle. 8 And the four beasts had each of them six wings about him; and they were full of eyes within: and they rest not day and night, saying, Holy, holy, holy, Lord God Almighty, which was, and is, and is to come.**

What struck me is that these creatures, created by

God, are all voluntarily praising and worshipping Him. Why. It is because He alone is worthy. One might ask, "What choice do they have?" That is the point. If one-third of the angelic host chose, by their free will, to abandon God and follow the rebel Satan, then those who remain also have free will. Those who chose to remain in His presence cannot help but gush praise to the One Who is worthy.

It is not only the creatures who were created by God that praise Him. The twenty-four elders also worship Him. Verses 9-10:

> 9 **And when those beasts give glory and honour and thanks to him that sat on the throne, who liveth for ever and ever,** 10 <u>**The four and twenty elders fall down before him that sat on the throne**</u>**, and worship him that liveth for ever and ever, and cast their crowns before the throne, saying,**

At a point in the not too distant future, all Creation will hear these words. Verse 11:

> 11 **Thou art worthy, O Lord, to receive glory and honour and power: for thou hast created all things, and for thy pleasure they are and were created.**

5

Revelation 5

So far, based upon the description in the previous chapter, the scene has been set. Now, John begins to describe the action upon the stage of his vision. Revelation 5: 1-4:

> 1 **And I saw in the right hand of him that sat on the throne a book written within and on the backside, sealed with seven seals. 2 And I saw a strong angel proclaiming with a loud voice, Who is worthy to open the book, and to loose the seals thereof? 3 And no man in heaven, nor in earth, neither under the earth, was able to open the book, neither to look thereon.**

So far, we know that the Tribulation is called "the time of Jacob's trouble" (Jer. 30:7). During these remaining seven years of testing, true Israel will be revealed while leaving those who are not true Israel to be judged. With these facts in mind, consider the following prophecy. Michael, like Gabriel, is an arch-angel who serves God and stands for the children of Israel. The following prophecy speaks about the judgment and deliverance. Daniel 12:1-4

> 1 **And at that time shall Michael stand up, the great prince which <u>standeth for the children of thy people</u>: and <u>there shall be a time of trouble</u>, such as never was since there was a nation even to that same time: and <u>at that time thy people shall be delivered, every one that shall be found written in the book</u>. 2 And many of them that sleep in the dust of the earth shall awake, some to everlast-ing life, and some to shame and ever-lasting contempt. 3 <u>And they that be wise shall shine as the brightness of the firmament; and they that turn many to righteousness as the stars for ever and ever</u>. 4 But thou, <u>O Daniel, shut up the words, and seal the book, even to the time of the end</u>: many shall run to and fro, and knowledge shall be increased.**

Those who turn people to the righteousness of God

will be like stars. Daniel is told to seal up this book until when? It is to be sealed until "the time of the end." The end of verse 4 says that people will be running to and fro in chaos and confusion. What does it mean by "and knowledge shall be increased?"

Wisdom is from God. Knowledge and science is from man. It is the natural inclination of man to come up with their own solutions and opinions. They strive to increase in their human knowledge; not in the Word of God. Paul warned Grace Believers about the same thing. Colossians 2:8-10

> 8 **Beware lest any man spoil you through philosophy and vain deceit, after the tradition of men, after the rudiments of the world, and not after Christ.** 9 **For in him dwelleth all the fulness of the Godhead bodily.** 10 **And ye are complete in him, which is the head of all principality and power:**

Above, the word *beware* is intended as a warning. It means *to be restrained or guarded, to be cautious as to something dangerous, injurious or improper.* Instead of being humble and submitting to the Word of God, men in their pride have come up with their own knowledge and solutions. We should all consider this as a warning. If any man have an ear, let him hear. In other words, if anyone has the ability to think, then let them think about this.

In Revelation, the use of numbers is important. The number of days in Creation including the day of rest is seven. The number seven is used to symbolize perfection. There are seven seals on this book and they are searching for the One Who is worthy to open them. John is grieved until He is found. The titles "Root of David" and "Lion of Judah" specifically refer to the Lord Jesus Christ. Verses 4-5:

> 4 **And I wept much, because no man was found worthy to open and to read the book, neither to look thereon. 5 And one of the elders saith unto me, Weep not: behold, <u>the Lion of the tribe of Juda, the Root of David, hath prevailed to open the book, and to loose the seven seals</u> thereof.**

Their search for Someone worthy comes to an end. There is another title given to Jesus Christ. Let us look in the Gospel of John. Look at the proclamation made by John the Baptist saying, "Behold the Lamb of God, which taketh away the sin of the world" (Jn. 1:29). The Apostle John was an eyewitness throughout Jesus' earthly ministry. He testifies, "And I saw, and bare record that this is the Son of God" (Jn. 1:34).

The title the Lamb of God is very important for Israel. Jesus Christ is both Israel's Messiah and their Passover Lamb. He appears center stage and takes the book from the One seated upon the throne. Many have asked, "Who is the One seated upon the throne? Is it God or is it Jesus Christ?" For me, the answer to that question is "Yes!" We know that Jesus is seated beside the Father. (See Psalm 110:1.) Stephen was the first martyr for the Gospel of the Kingdom. At his stoning Luke records his words. Acts 7:55-56:

> 55 **But he, being full of the Holy Ghost, looked up stedfastly into heaven, and saw the glory of God, and Jesus standing on the right hand of God, 56 And said, <u>Behold, I see the heavens opened, and the Son of man standing on the right hand of God.</u>**

We know that the Father and Son are One and they are seated together. We should focus our attention on the appearance of the Lamb Who is the only One worthy. Shortly, we will see Who is seated upon the throne.

There is additional prophetic symbolism, but we should not let it detract our attention from the main points. It may be entertaining to consider the meaning of the seven horns and seven eyes, but the point is that Jesus Christ took the book from Whom? Jesus took it from the One Who sat upon the throne. That answers our previous question. Verses 6-7:

> 6 And I beheld, and, lo, in the midst of the throne and of the four beasts, and in the midst of the elders, stood <u>a Lamb as it had been slain</u>, having seven horns and seven eyes, which are the seven Spirits of God sent forth into all the earth. 7 And he came and took the book out of the right hand of him that sat upon the throne.

The Lamb receives the book and when He does, praise erupts. Verses 8-9:

> 8 And when he had taken the book, the four beasts and four and twenty elders fell down before the Lamb, having every one of them harps, and golden vials full of odours, which are the prayers of saints. 9 And they sung a new song, saying, <u>Thou art worthy to take the book, and to open the seals thereof: for thou wast slain, and hast redeemed us to God by thy blood</u> out of every kindred, and tongue, and people, and nation;

In the next verse, this particular praise applies specifically to true Israel. Following the Tribulation which is the testing of true Israel, those who endure to the end will receive salvation and God's blessings. Notice what God will do for them. Verse 10:

10 And hast made us unto our God kings and priests: and we shall reign on the earth.

First, they will be kings and priests. Second, they will reign with Him. Where is that? It will be on the earth. Everything about Israel's future is earthly-based. The Kingdom will be established on earth. Jerusalem will be its capital. There, David's throne will be established forever by Jesus the King. God's promises do not change. Exodus 19:3-6:

3 And Moses went up unto God, and the LORD called unto him out of the mountain, saying, Thus shalt thou <u>say to the house of Jacob, and tell the children of Israel;</u> 4 Ye have seen what I did unto the Egyptians, and how I bare you on eagles' wings, and brought you unto myself. 5 Now therefore, <u>if ye will obey my voice indeed, and keep my covenant, then ye shall be a peculiar treasure unto me above all people</u>: for all the

earth is mine: 6 And ye shall be unto me a kingdom of priests, and an holy nation. These are the words which thou shalt speak unto the children of Israel.

Did you notice the if-then conditional statement above? If Israel obeys God and keeps the Mosaic Covenant, then two things will happen. First, Israel will be a peculiar or unique treasure among all the other nations on earth. Second, they will be a kingdom of priests and a nation separated unto God to serve Him in His Kingdom.

John continues with details of his vision. Revelation 5:11-12:

11 And I beheld, and I heard the voice of many angels round about the throne and the beasts and the elders: and the number of them was ten thousand times ten thousand, and thousands of thousands; 12 Saying with a loud voice, <u>Worthy is the Lamb that was slain to receive power, and riches, and wisdom, and strength, and honour, and glory, and blessing.</u>

In recognition of all that Jesus Christ accomplished on earth, all of the innumerable heavenly host cry out with a loud voice. They proclaim that the Lamb is worthy. The praise continues. Verses 13-14:

> 13 And every creature which is in heaven, and on the earth, and under the earth, and such as are in the sea, and all that are in them, heard I saying, Blessing, and honour, and glory, and power, be unto him that sitteth upon the throne, and unto the Lamb for ever and ever.

> 14 And the four beasts said, Amen. And the four and twenty elders fell down and worshipped him that liveth for ever and ever.

Here are some other confirmations of what will happen at the conclusion of God's restoration.

Isaiah 45:23-25:

> 23 I have sworn by myself, the word is gone out of my mouth in righteousness, and shall not return, That unto me every knee shall bow, every tongue shall swear. 24 Surely, shall one say, in the LORD have I righteousness and strength: even to him shall men come;

and all that are incensed against him shall be ashamed. 25 In the LORD shall all the seed of Israel be justified, and shall glory.

Romans 14:11:

11 For it is written, As I live, saith the Lord, every knee shall bow to me, and every tongue shall confess to God.

Philippians 2:10-11:

10 That at the name of Jesus every knee should bow, of things in heaven, and things in earth, and things under the earth; 11 And that every tongue should confess that Jesus Christ is Lord, to the glory of God the Father.

Since before the beginning, this has been God's plan. He will restore His Creation and everyone, both the living and the dead, will ultimately proclaim that Jesus Christ is Lord!

6

Revelation 6

A series of events occur at the breaking of the seven seals. John sees how these events affect the earth and those that dwell upon it. Remember, believers who were saved by the Gospel of Grace were removed at the Rapture. These events cannot apply to them. Revelation 6:1-2:

> 1 **And I saw when the Lamb opened <u>one of the seals</u>, and I heard, as it were the noise of thunder, one of the four beasts saying, Come and see. 2 And I saw, and behold a white horse: and he that sat on him had a bow; and a crown was given unto him: and he went forth conquering, and to conquer.**

Let us take a look at the word *conquer.* It means *to subdue by physical force until all opposition is overcome;*

to vanquish; to take possession by violent means in order to gain dominion or sovereignty or power over an enemy. It is usually the general who rides the white horse and leads the battle. Many believe that this is Jesus Christ Who is riding this white horse. I do not believe this is the case as others also ride white horses. Jesus will appear towards the end of the great battle riding a white horse. (See Revelation 19:11-14.)

There will be wars and battles fought against the spiritual realm. It continues with the opening of the second seal. Revelation 6: 3-4:

> 3 **And when he had opened <u>the second seal</u>, I heard the second beast say, Come and see. 4 And there went out another horse that was red: and power was given to him that sat thereon to take peace [away] from the earth, and that they should kill one another: and there was given unto him a great sword.**

The Tribulation is sometimes referred to as "the Day of the Lord." It is the day of His wrath and judgment. Paul, speaking to Grace Believers, explains the coming of this day that they will avoid. 1 Thessalonians 5:2-3:

> 2 **For yourselves know perfectly that <u>the</u>**

day of the Lord so cometh as a thief in the night. 3 For when they shall say, Peace and safety; then sudden destruction cometh upon them, as travail upon a woman with child; and they shall not escape.

The third seal is broken. Another horse represents scarcity of food and the beginning of hunger. Revelation 6:5-6:

5 And when he had opened the third seal, I heard the third beast say, Come and see. And I beheld, and lo a black horse; and he that sat on him had a pair of balances in his hand. 6 And I heard a voice in the midst of the four beasts say, A measure of wheat for a penny, and three measures of barley for a penny; and see thou hurt not the oil and the wine.

In the next seal, there will be death for more than a quarter of the earth's population. There will be uprisings and revolts, mass confusion where many will be killed. Verses 7-8:

7 And when he had opened the fourth seal, I heard the voice of the fourth

beast say, Come and see. 8 And I looked, and behold a pale horse: and his name that sat on him was Death, and Hell followed with him. And power was given unto them over the fourth part of the earth, to kill with sword, and with hunger, and with death, and with the beasts of the earth.

With the fifth seal, we see something different. Those who serve the Lord during the Tribulation will be recognized. These are the faithful who were slain because they continued to preach the Gospel of the Kingdom. In Matthew 24, Jesus answered His disciples question, "Tell us, when shall these things be? and what shall be the sign of thy coming, and of the end of the world?" (Matt. 24:3). Towards the end of that chapter, Jesus makes this statement. Matthew 24:13-14:

13 But he that shall endure unto the end, the same shall be saved. 14 And this gospel of the kingdom shall be preached in all the world for a witness unto all nations; and then shall the end come.

To these witnesses who brought that testimony, John writes in Revelation 6:9-11:

9 And when he had opened the fifth seal, I saw under the altar the souls of them that were slain for the word of God, and for the testimony which they held: 10 And they cried with a loud voice, saying, How long, O Lord, holy and true, dost thou not judge and avenge our blood on them that dwell on the earth? 11 And white robes were given unto every one of them; and it was said unto them, that they should rest yet for a little season, until their fellowservants also and their brethren, that should be killed as they were, should be fulfilled.

The book of Revelation is the conclusion or fulfillment of all the outstanding prophecies in the Bible. It is for that reason that we make reference to them. God will always do what He said He will do. "For I am the LORD, I change not . . ." (Mal. 3:6) Although there has been great turmoil throughout the history of the world, nothing like this has been or will ever be. Chronologically, we are progressing towards the end of the seven-year period. Jesus Christ breaks the sixth seal. Verses 12-17:

12 And I beheld when he had opened the sixth seal, and, lo, there was a great

earthquake; and the sun became black as sackcloth of hair, and the moon became as blood; 13 And the stars of heaven fell unto the earth, even as a fig tree casteth her untimely figs, when she is shaken of a mighty wind. 14 And the heaven departed as a scroll when it is rolled together; and every mountain and island were moved out of their places. 15 And the kings of the earth, and the great men, and the rich men, and the chief captains, and the mighty men, and every bondman, and every free man, hid themselves in the dens and in the rocks of the mountains; 16 And said to the mountains and rocks, Fall on us, and hide us from the face of him that sitteth on the throne, and from the wrath of the Lamb: 17 For the great day of his wrath is come; and who shall be able to stand?

We will read about the breaking of the seventh and final seal in Revelations 8.

7

Revelation 7

Seals can be placed upon documents for security of their content and to prevent them from being opened. Other seals can be placed upon the documents. They simply provide credentials as to the authenticity and authority of the document. I believe the seal from God was placed upon the document providing instructions to the four angels who stand on the four corners of the earth. Remember that the word *angel* comes from the Greek word *angelos* meaning *messenger*. These are spiritual beings that God dispatches to bring messages and to execute His judgments. Revelations 7:1-3

> 1 **And after these things I saw four angels standing on the four corners of the earth, holding the four winds of the earth, that the wind should not blow on the earth, nor on the sea, nor on any tree.**

2 And I saw <u>another angel</u> ascending from the east, <u>having the seal of the living God</u>: and he cried with a loud voice to the four angels, to whom it was given to hurt the earth and the sea, 3 Saying, Hurt not the earth, neither the sea, nor the trees, till we have sealed the servants of our God in their foreheads.

The other angel is giving official instructions to the four angels. They are not to begin their judgment upon the earth until the "servants of God" are marked or sealed on their foreheads.

How many of these servants are there? John hears the number. Verse 4:

4 And I heard the number of them which were sealed: and there were sealed an hundred and forty and four thousand of all the tribes of the children of Israel.

The ones being marked or sealed are true Israel. In the following verses, we find that there are twelve thousand from each of the Twelve Tribes. Verses 5-8:

5 Of the tribe of Juda were sealed twelve thousand. Of the tribe of Reuben were

sealed twelve thousand. Of the tribe of Gad were sealed twelve thousand. 6 Of the tribe of Aser were sealed twelve thousand. Of the tribe of Nepthalim were sealed twelve thousand. Of the tribe of Manasses were sealed twelve thousand. 7 Of the tribe of Simeon were sealed twelve thousand. Of the tribe of Levi were sealed twelve thousand. Of the tribe of Issachar were sealed twelve thousand. 8 Of the tribe of Zabulon were sealed twelve thousand. Of the tribe of Joseph were sealed twelve thousand. Of the tribe of Benjamin were sealed twelve thousand.

The above one hundred forty-four thousand represent true Israel, but there are also Gentiles who will endure as well. Verses 9-10:

9 After this I beheld, and, lo, a great multitude, which no man could number, of all nations, and kindreds, and people, and tongues, stood before the throne, and before the Lamb, clothed with white robes, and palms in their hands; 10 And cried with a loud voice, saying, Salvation to our God which sitteth upon the throne, and unto the

Lamb.

The specific number of these Gentiles, non-Jews, is not given. We are left with only the words "a great multitude."

Let us look at the promise that God made directly to Abraham concerning the Gentiles. Genesis 12:2-3:

> 2 **And I will make of thee a great nation, and I will bless thee, and make thy name great; and thou shalt be a blessing:** 3 **And <u>I will bless them that bless thee, and curse him that curseth thee</u>: and in thee shall all families of the earth be blessed.**

Verse 2 has to do with God blessing Abraham and his children. However, verse 3 is speaking about the other nations. If they bless Israel especially in their time of trials, then God will bless them. However, if they curse or bring anguish upon them, then God will curse them. When will this happen? In the end times and during the Tribulation. It is through Abraham that "all the families of the earth" will eventually be blessed.

Again, the praises of those who surround the

throne break forth. Revelation 7:11-12:

> 11 **And all the angels stood round about the throne, and about the elders and the four beasts, and fell before the throne on their faces, and worshipped God, 12 Saying, Amen: Blessing, and glory, and wisdom, and thanksgiving, and honour, and power, and might, be unto our God for ever and ever. Amen.**

One of the twenty-four elders asks John a question. Verse 13:

> 13 **And one of the elders answered, saying unto me, What are these which are arrayed in white robes? and whence [from where] came they?**

John does not know the answer to the question and the angel explains. Verse 14:

> 14 **And I said unto him, Sir, thou knowest. And he said to me, These are they which came out of great tribulation, and have washed their robes, and made them white in the blood of the Lamb.**

These are the martyrs that are killed during the great

tribulation which is the last half of the seven years. The angel continues by telling John about the blessings these martyrs will receive. Those who proclaim the righteousness of God by preaching the Gospel of the Kingdom will be killed. Verses 15-16:

> 15 **Therefore are they before the throne of God, and serve him day and night in his temple: and he that sitteth on the throne shall dwell among them. 16 They shall hunger no more, neither thirst any more; neither shall the sun light on them, nor any heat.**

The angel describes the blessing that will surround them following the close of the Tribulation. Verse 17:

> 17 **For the Lamb which is in the midst of the throne shall feed them, and shall lead them unto living fountains of waters: and God shall wipe away all tears from their eyes.**

8

Revelation 8

We read about the six seals upon the book. The One Who is worthy, Jesus Christ, is now going to open the seventh and final seal. Revelation 8:1:

> **1 And when he had opened the seventh seal, there was silence in heaven about the space of half an hour.**

All Creation stands still. There is a silent reverence for a brief span of time and, following this silence, the action resumes.

Seven angels or messengers stand and watch as another angel offers incense before the throne. Verses 2-5:

> **2 And I saw the seven angels which stood before God; and to them were**

given seven trumpets. 3 And another angel came and stood at the altar, having a golden censer; and <u>there was given unto him much incense</u>, that he should offer it with <u>the prayers of all saints</u> upon the golden altar which was before the throne.

This incense is offered along with "the prayers of all the saints" before the throne. King David wrote about his prayers comparing them to incense being presented before God. Psalms 141:1-2:

1 LORD, I cry unto thee: make haste unto me; give ear unto my voice, when I cry unto thee. 2 Let my prayer be set forth before thee as incense . . .

Picture the smoke from the incense rising before God. Revelation 8:4:

4 And the smoke of the incense, which came with the prayers of the saints, ascended up before God out of the angel's hand.

Notice what the angel with the censer, the container of burning incense, does with it. We should think about all the Jews who pray for the peace of

Jerusalem. There is only one way that peace can come to Jerusalem. The Lord God Almighty must bring it. In order for Him to do this, He must complete His judgments. The following action will get the attention of everyone on earth. Verse 5.

> 5 And **the angel took the censer,** and filled it with fire of the altar, **and cast it into the earth:** and there were voices, and thunderings, and lightnings, and an earthquake.

The seven angels who were waiting and watching for this to be completed now prepare. Verse 6:

> 6 And the seven angels which had the seven trumpets prepared themselves to sound.

Before we move to the judgments of the seven trumpets, some may ask, "Why is God doing this?" In the first chapter of Romans, Paul presents a brilliant argument for the justification of God's judgment upon humanity. His inspired words provide God's conclusion. Romans 1:28-32:

> 28 And even as **they did not like to retain God in their knowledge,** God gave them over to a reprobate mind, to do

**those things which are not convenient
[acceptable]; 29 Being filled with all un-
righteousness, fornication, wickedness,
covetousness, maliciousness; full of
envy, murder, debate, deceit, malignity;
whisperers, 30 Backbiters, haters of
God, despiteful, proud, boasters, inven-
tors of evil things, disobedient to par-
ents, 31 Without understanding, cove-
nant-breakers, without natural affec-
tion, implacable, unmerciful: 32 Who
knowing the judgment of God, that
they which commit such things are worthy of death, not only do the same, but
have pleasure in them that do them.**

Paul shows that God is justified in His actions to
judge those who do evil. They reject God and His offers for salvation. By doing so, they have sealed their
own destiny.

During the Age of Grace, introduced by the
Apostle Paul, God withholds His judgment while He
offers amnesty to all individuals through the Gospel
of Grace. Believers receive salvation immediately
upon their faith in His Son's death, burial, and resurrection. Salvation by grace through faith in the completed work of Jesus Christ is available to both Jew
and Gentile alike. At the Rapture, however, God's

offer of salvation by grace through faith alone is withdrawn. Therefore, it is different for those who are saved by the Gospel of the Kingdom. They must continually demonstrate their faith in the Messiah and the Son of God. They must do good works and their faith must endure until the end. Upon the return of their Messiah, they will receive their salvation and God's blessings.

This is so important, I will say it again. For the Jews, their Messiah came to confirm the promises made to *their* fathers: Abraham, Isaac, and Jacob. (See Romans 15:8.) Like Peter, they are to confess the following to Jesus. ". . . Thou art the Christ, the Son of the living God" (Matt. 16:16). In addition to believing that Jesus Christ is the Messiah and the Son of God, they are to follow the Apostles. Jesus commanded the Apostles to, "Go ye therefore, and teach all nations, baptizing them in the name of the Father, and of the Son, and of the Holy Ghost: Teaching them to observe all things whatsoever I have commanded you" (Matt. 28:19-20). The word observes means to keep the Law and His commandments by *doing* them. They must continue to follow the Law. Because of their long history of repeatedly losing their faith, they must continue to prove their faith. Writing to Kingdom Believers, the Apostle James wrote, "For as the body without the spirit is dead, so faith without works is dead also" (Jas. 2:26). Concerning the end times, Jesus told His disciples that salvation will be given to those who endure to the end. Matthew 24:13-14:

> 13 **But he that shall endure unto the end, the same shall be saved. 14 And this gospel of the kingdom shall be preached in all the world for a witness unto all nations; and then shall the end come.**

The book of Revelation was written to those who want to endure to the end in order to receive their salvation. They will also see their King and His Kingdom established forever.

At this point, we begin another series of seven events. These occur upon the sounding of each of the seven trumpets. Here is the first. Revelation 8:7:

> 7 <u>**The first angel**</u> **sounded, and there followed hail and fire mingled with blood, and they were cast upon the earth: and the third part of trees was burnt up, and all green grass was burnt up.**

The children of Adam had received the bounty of God's Creation found in the sea and the air, and upon the verdant earth. Genesis 1:26-28:

26 And God said, Let us make man in our image, after our likeness: and let them have dominion over the fish of the sea, and over the fowl of the air, and over the cattle, and over all the earth, and over every creeping thing that creepeth upon the earth. 27 So God created man in his own image, in the image of God created he him; male and female created he them. 28 And God blessed them, and God said unto them, Be fruitful, and multiply, and replenish the earth, and subdue it: and have dominion over the fish of the sea, and over the fowl of the air, and over every living thing that moveth upon the earth.

In God's judgments, He begins to withdraw not what was man's by right, but what was his by privilege.

He levied judgment upon the sea. Revelation 8:8-9:

8 And <u>the second angel</u> sounded, and as it were a great mountain burning with fire was cast into the sea: and the third part of the sea became blood; 9 And the third part of the creatures which were in the sea, and had life, died; and the third

part of the ships were destroyed.

The seas provide transportation and food. In the next trumpet, God extends His judgment to the inland waterways. This is the drinkable water needed by man for survival. Verses 10-11:

> 10 **And <u>the third angel</u> sounded, and there fell a great star from heaven, burning as it were a lamp, and it fell upon the third part of the rivers, and upon the fountains of waters; 11 And the name of the star is called Wormwood: and the third part of the waters became wormwood; and many men died of the waters, because they were made bitter.**

Each step that God takes in removing the blessings of Creation, are designed to make mankind turn away from their wickedness and turn to God. They are to repent which means do an about-face, leaving their wickedness behind, and turning to God.

God is gradually dismantling the life-supporting structure of His Creation. In the fourth judgment, He removes a portion of the sun, the moon, and the stars. Verse 12:

12 **And <u>the fourth angel</u> sounded, and**

the third part of the sun was smitten, and the third part of the moon, and the third part of the stars; so as the third part of them was darkened, and the day shone not for a third part of it, and the night likewise.

An angelic announcement is made proclaiming *woe* to all who dwell on the earth. The word *woe* means *grief, sorrow, misery; great calamity.* This applies to all the Jews and Gentiles who are upon the earth at this time. Verse 13:

13 And I beheld, and heard an angel flying through the midst of heaven, saying with a loud voice, Woe, woe, woe, to the inhabiters of the earth by reason of the other voices of the trumpet of the three angels, which are yet to sound!

Four trumpeters have sounded. The above announcement is made before the sounding of the last three trumpeters.

9

Revelation 9

From the closing verse in the last chapter, we can anticipate that circumstances on earth will get much worse. The fifth angel sounds his trumpet. Revelation 9:1-2:

> 1 And <u>the fifth angel</u> sounded, and I saw a star fall from heaven unto the earth: and to him was given the key of the bottomless pit. 2 And he opened the bottomless pit; and there arose a smoke out of the pit, as the smoke of a great furnace; and the sun and the air were darkened by reason of the smoke of the pit.

The words "the bottomless pit" are mentioned together in the Bible seven times. All of these references are found in the book of Revelation. The description of "the smoke of a great furnace" paints a picture of hopelessness and despair. Once "the bottomless pit" is opened, those within are provided access to the earthly realm.

This judgment will last for five months. This time, punishment is directed not on Creation, but upon men who will be tormented near unto death. Verses 3-6:

> 3 **And there came out of the smoke locusts upon the earth: and unto them was given power, as the scorpions of the earth have power. 4 And it was commanded them that they should not hurt the grass of the earth, neither any green thing, neither any tree; but only those men which have not the seal of God in their foreheads. 5 And to them <u>it was given that they should not kill them, but that they should be tormented five months</u>: and their torment was as the torment of a scorpion, when he striketh a man. 6 <u>And in those days shall men seek death, and shall not find it; and shall desire to die, and death shall flee from them</u>.**

Conditions become so bad, that men desire to die, but death will evade them. Therefore, the inhabitants of the earth are forced to suffer the judgment. The tormentors are shaped like locusts but armored for battle. These are creatures which no man has seen before. They are not man-made drones as their origin is from within "the bottomless pit." John gives us their description. Verses 7-10:

> 7 **And the shapes of the locusts were like unto horses prepared unto battle; and on their heads were as it were crowns like gold, and their faces were as the faces of men. 8 And they had hair as the hair of women, and their teeth were as the teeth of lions. 9 And they had breastplates, as it were breastplates of iron; and the sound of their wings was as the sound of chariots of many horses running to battle. 10 And they had tails like unto scorpions, and there were stings in their tails: and their power was to hurt men five months.**

Some Bible students become frustrated as their curiosity is not being satisfied. I like to tell them that the Bible does not tell us what we want to know. It tells us what God wants us to know.

Over this battalion of locust-like creatures, there is a king or ruler. We are given his name in both

Hebrew and Greek. In Hebrew, it means *Destruction* and in Greek it means *Destroyer*. Verse 11:

> 11 **And they had a king over them, which is the angel of the bottomless pit, whose name in the Hebrew tongue is Abaddon, but in the Greek tongue hath his name Apollyon.**

Apollyon is a fallen angel, a ruler over the demonic forces unleashed from the bottomless pit. He serves within Satan's evil hierarchy. This event is the result of the fifth trumpet. There are two more trumpets in this series. Verse 12:

> 12 **One woe is past; and, behold, there come two woes more hereafter.**

The timing of the judgments is designed to coincide with the conclusion of the seven-year Tribulation. As each trumpet is blown, the woe escalates. Verses 13-15:

> 13 **And <u>the sixth angel</u> sounded, and I heard a voice from the four horns of the golden altar which is before God, 14 Saying to the sixth angel which had the trumpet, Loose the four angels which are bound in the great river Euphrates.**

15 And the four angels were loosed, which were prepared for an hour, and a day, and a month, and a year, for to slay the third part of men.

With this trumpet, the four angels which were bound are released. We will look at these four angels in greater detail momentarily. We are told that their mission will be prolonged for thirteen months and a day. That mission is "to slay the third part of men" living upon the earth.

These four angels were once bound but now are free. They will direct an army to achieve their purpose. John overhears the number of this army and shares the number with us. The number is two hundred million. The description of the soldiers and their horses defy comparison to any known creature. These are fearsome and terrifying adversaries. Verses 16-17:

16 And the number of the army of the horsemen were two hundred thousand thousand: and I heard the number of them. 17 And thus I saw the horses in the vision, and them that sat on them, having breastplates of fire, and of jacinth, and brimstone: and the heads of the horses were as the heads of lions; and

out of their mouths issued fire and smoke and brimstone.

These horses or modes of conveyance have heads like lions and from their mouths they breathe out smoke and brimstone which is molten Sulphur.

It is by these means that their mission to eradicate a third of mankind is carried out. These creatures are fearsome foes. Verses 18-19:

> 18 **By these three was the third part of men killed, by the fire, and by the smoke, and by the brimstone, which issued out of their mouths.** 19 **For their power is in their mouth, and in their tails: for their tails were like unto serpents, and had heads, and with them they do hurt.**

Remember, the Creator is trying to motivate mankind to repent and turn back to God. We are told that they will not. Their minds are obstinate and set against God. They will continue in their pride and worship idols made by their hands. They will not repent but continue in their abominations. Verses 20-21:

> 20 **And the rest of the men which were**

not killed by these plagues yet repented not of the works of their hands, that they should not worship devils, and idols of gold, and silver, and brass, and stone, and of wood: which neither can see, nor hear, nor walk: 21 Neither repented they of their murders, nor of their sorceries, nor of their fornication, nor of their thefts.

10

Revelation 10

Many things that John witnesses are supernatural and difficult to picture. He does the best he can to record what he sees and hears. In the following, I believe that the angel or messenger from heaven, whose face shown like the sun, is the Lord Jesus Christ. He has acted as God's messenger before. However, because it is not specifically stated, this would be only an assumption. Revelation 10:1-3:

> 1 **And I saw another mighty angel come down from heaven, clothed with a cloud: and a rainbow was upon his head, and his face was as it were the sun, and his feet as pillars of fire:** 2 **And he had in his hand a little book open: and he set his right foot upon the sea, and his left foot on the earth,** 3 **And cried with a loud voice, as when a lion**

roareth: and when he had cried, seven thunders uttered their voices.

John is prevented from writing down the words spoken to him by the seven thunders. Verse 4:

4 **And when the seven thunders had uttered their voices, I was about to write: and I heard a voice from heaven saying unto me, Seal up those things which the seven thunders uttered, and write them not.**

This messenger who is standing upon the sea and the earth makes a proclamation that time is complete. They have arrived at the end time and time should be no more. Verses 5-7:

5 **And the angel which I saw stand upon the sea and upon the earth lifted up his hand to heaven, 6 And sware by him that liveth for ever and ever, who created heaven, and the things that therein are, and the earth, and the things that therein are, and the sea, and the things which are therein, that there should be time no longer:**

All that God has declared through the prophets is

now complete.

> 7 But in the days of the voice of the seventh angel, when he shall begin to sound, the mystery of God should be finished, as he hath declared to his servants the prophets.

The Apostle John is directed to obtain "the little book" from the angel. Verse 8:

> 8 And the voice which I heard from heaven spake unto me again, and said, Go and take the little book which is open in the hand of the angel which standeth upon the sea and upon the earth.

When he does so, he is given another command. He is to take "the little book" from the angel and eat it. Verse 9:

> 9 And I went unto the angel, and said unto him, Give me the little book. And he said unto me, Take it, and eat it up; and it shall make thy belly bitter, but it shall be in thy mouth sweet as honey.

John notes that it is "sweet as honey" in his mouth,

but afterwards, it is bitter in his stomach. Some people consume knowledge like it is food. John had just received revelation from God. He heard it and digested it. Verse 10:

> 10 **And I took the little book out of the angel's hand, and ate it up; and it was in my mouth sweet as honey: and as soon as I had eaten it, my belly was bitter.**

He is instructed to prophesy not only to Israel, but also to the Gentile nations and their kings. I believe the revelation that John was given would not be well received by "many peoples." This may be the cause of the bitterness or sorrow within him. Verse 11:

> 11 **And he said unto me, Thou must prophesy again before many peoples, and nations, and tongues, and kings.**

11

Revelation 11

What the Apostle John sees in his visions is difficult to put into words. We are told that he is given a reed which is grass-like but has a hollow stem like bamboo. John is told to measure the temple, the altar, and the worshippers. Revelation 11:1:

> 1 **And there was given me a reed like unto a rod: and the angel stood, saying, Rise, and measure the temple of God, and the altar, and them that worship therein.**

What he is seeing is the new Jerusalem which is presently in heaven. The temple of God will be the focal point. However, he is instructed not to measure beyond that. Verse 2:

> 2 **But the court which is without the tem-**

ple leave out, and measure it not; for it is given unto the Gentiles: and the holy city shall they tread under foot forty and two months.

The second Temple in Jerusalem which was destroyed in A.D. 70, had a courtyard that surrounded it. John is specifically told not to measure it. I suspect that it is going to be far greater in size than its predecessor. There is much information I need to summarize here. It is examined in depth in *Letters To Theophilus* and *The Glorious Destiny of Israel*. We cannot really understand the end without understanding what comes before it. What occurs in Revelation is the fulfillment of all the books that precede it. At this time, there are only two groups of people: Jews and non-Jews. The latter are referred to as the Gentiles or nations. We are told that these Gentiles will trample the area for forty-two months. This length of time is significant as it represents the last three and one-half years. Briefly, God gave the prophet Daniel a timeline. Jesus refers to it in Matthew 24.

Daniel, while in exile in Babylon, beseeches God to restore the holy city Jerusalem. Gabriel brings God's response to Daniel which far exceeds his request. Look at what God will complete by the end of these "seventy weeks." I added numbers in brackets to fully comprehend the extent of this. Daniel 9:24:

24 <u>**Seventy weeks are determined**</u> **upon thy people and upon thy holy city, [1] to finish the transgression, and [2] to make an end of sins, and [3] to make reconciliation for iniquity, and [4] to bring in everlasting righteousness, and [5] to seal up the vision and prophecy, and [6] to anoint the most Holy.**

The seventy weeks are actually seventy weeks-of-years. In other words, the total time is not seventy years, but four hundred ninety years. Daniel had asked God when He would restore Jerusalem from its present devastation. Yet, God's response to Daniel's prayer gave him much more. God told him when the new Jerusalem would be established. At the four hundred eighty-third year, the Messiah is cutoff and the prophetic timeline is suspended. The Age of Grace deals with the Gentiles. The Age of Grace concludes with the Rapture and Daniel's timeline resumes. The seven remaining years, called the Tribulation, will test true Israel. The Gospel of Grace is withdrawn at the Rapture and preaching of the Gospel of the Kingdom resumes.

In Matthew 24, Jesus confirms the validity of Daniel's timeline which we are presently studying in Revelation. Speaking of the end time, Jesus explains to His disciples. Matthew 24:14:

14 And this gospel of the kingdom shall be preached in all the world for a witness unto all nations; and then shall the end come.

We can be confident that the gospel being preached in the end time is the Gospel of the Kingdom. Some might ask, "How is this gospel going to be preached and who will preach it?" God will provide two witnesses. Now, witnesses are generally those who have seen or heard something about which they testify. Revelations 11:3:

3 And I will give power unto my two witnesses, and they shall prophesy a thousand two hundred and threescore days, clothed in sackcloth.

We will deal with the two witnesses momentarily, but let us nail down this time period. The Tribulation is a period of seven years, right? Half of this would be three and one-half years, right? Well, this same three and one-half years is referred to above as one thousand two hundred and sixty days. In other places, it is referred to as forty-two months. This is the same period of time and, in this case, it is referring to the last half of the Tribulation.

Many people have speculated on who these two witnesses are. We will look at two cases and I will leave it to you to decide. It has been suggested that the two witnesses will be Enoch and Elijah. They were both taken up into heaven without dying. (See Genesis 5 and 2 Kings 2.) At the conclusion of their Tribulation ministry, both of these witnesses will be killed. In Hebrews, a book written to Kingdom Believers, we read that ". . . it is appointed unto men once to die, but after this the judgment" (Heb. 9:27). Alternatively, others suggest that Moses and Elijah will be the two witnesses. They argue that, first, during their earthly ministry they displayed miraculous powers. Moses turned water into blood and displayed incredible signs. Furthermore, he called down multiple plagues upon those who stood against God. Elijah also did many signs and wonders including calling down fire and withholding rain. Second, both of them were present at Jesus' Transfiguration. (See Matthew 17.) These two prophets are the most revered by the Jewish people. If any prophets will be able to reach them, then it would be these two mighty men of God.

The two witnesses have a difficult job before them. In the following verse, they are referred to as "the two olive trees" and "the two candlesticks." The olive has always been symbolic of God's peace and the candlestick as bearing light in the darkness. However, the important point is not why these two items are so called. It is the location of the two items. They are standing before God. Verse 4:

> 4 **These are the two olive trees, and the two candlesticks standing before the God of the earth.**

These two mean business. The time is drawing to a close and God is giving mankind one last opportunity to repent for their sins and rebellion against Him. Verses 5-6:

> 5 **And if any man will hurt them, fire proceedeth out of their mouth, and devoureth their enemies: and if any man will hurt them, he must in this manner be killed.** 6 **These have power to shut heaven, that it rain not in the days of their prophecy: and have power over waters to turn them to blood, and to smite the earth with all plagues, as often as they will.**

These men are powerful and they will preach the Gospel of the Kingdom for the remaining three and one-half years. One might ask, "Why is it this length of time?"

The answer to that question has to do with Daniel's prophetic timeline. The Jews calculate their year as three hundred sixty days. The other days accumulate for religious festivals and holidays. Again, the last half of the Tribulation is "a thousand two hundred and threescore days" (v. 3). This period of time coincides with the flood of Gentiles. They are described as ". . . the people of the prince that shall come [and] shall destroy the city and the sanctuary; and the end thereof shall be with a flood, and unto the end of the war desolations are determined" (Dan. 9:26). For this reason, John is told not to measure the courtyard because " . . . it is given unto the Gentiles: and the holy city shall they tread under foot forty and two months . . ." (Rev. 11:2). This is the last half of the Tribulation.

Let us look at Daniel's prophecy again. He is told that the Messiah will "be cut off, but not for himself: and the people of the prince that shall come shall destroy the city and the sanctuary . . ." This "prince" is the Antichrist. Have you ever seen a video of people leaving a full stadium or streaming onto the field after the game? It looks like the flood of water. This verse continues ". . . and the end thereof shall be with a flood, and unto the end of the war desolations are determined" (Dan. 9:26). Be careful. The word "and" means consecutively but not necessarily concurrent.

Consider this example. John Alden was born in England and died in the Massachusetts Colony. The two events happened in the order stated, but not at the same time. In a moment, you will see why I am telling you this.

Many people are aware that, following the Rapture, the Tribulation begins with the Antichrist signing or confirming a covenant for seven years. It mentions two separate events, but they do not happen at the same time. Here is the first part. Daniel 9:27:

> 27 **And he shall confirm the covenant with many for one week: . . .**

One week is actually one week of seven years. Therefore, a seven-year covenant is created. It is confirmed by "many" nations allowing the Jews to return to their homeland in safety. At the mid-point or halfway through this seven-year covenant, something happens. The Antichrist will break the covenant. Here is the remainder of verse 27:

> **. . . and in the midst of the week he shall cause the sacrifice and the oblation to cease, and for the overspreading of abominations he shall make it desolate, even until the consummation, and that**

determined shall be poured upon the desolate.

This is when the flood of people pour into Jerusalem and the two witnesses appear. This craziness occurs for three and one-half years "until the consummation."

With this explanation, we can return to our text. The fate of these two witnesses has been determined. They will be killed. Picture this event being broadcast live with interviews of the killers, who are cheered as heroes, and eyewitnesses. Verses 7-10:

> 7 **And when they shall have finished their testimony, the beast that ascendeth out of the bottomless pit shall make war against them, and shall overcome them, and kill them.** 8 **And their dead bodies shall lie in the street of the great city, which spiritually is called Sodom and Egypt, where also our Lord was crucified.** 9 **And they of the people and kindreds and tongues and nations shall see their dead bodies three days and an half, and shall not suffer [allow] their dead bodies to be put in graves.** 10 **And they that dwell upon the earth shall rejoice over them, and make**

merry, and shall send gifts one to another; because these two prophets tormented them that dwelt on the earth.

The bodies of these witnesses are left to rot as they challenged the government of the Antichrist. However, the world is surprised by what follows. Verses 11-13:

> 11 And after three days and an half the Spirit of life from God entered into them, and they stood upon their feet; and great fear fell upon them which saw them. 12 And they heard a great voice from heaven saying unto them, Come up hither. And they ascended up to heaven in a cloud; and their enemies beheld them. 13 And the same hour was there a great earthquake, and the tenth part of the city fell, and in the earthquake were slain of men seven thousand: and the remnant were affrighted, and gave glory to the God of heaven.

The rebels who were slain numbered seven thousand. Israel who is true and faithful are called "the remnant." They rejoice and glorify God. They are those saved by the Gospel of the Kingdom. It is to them who the Apostle Peter wrote, "But the word of the Lord endureth for ever. And this is the word which by the gospel is preached unto you" (1 Pet. 1:25). Verse 14:

14 **The second woe is past; and, behold, the third woe cometh quickly.**

Like a theatrical performance, one act ends and the next one begins. The seventh, in any biblical series, is usually the last. As with this scenario, it signals completion. Verse 15:

15 **And the seventh angel sounded; and there were great voices in heaven, saying, The kingdoms of this world are become the kingdoms of our Lord, and of his Christ; and he shall reign for ever and ever.**

Everything is going according to plan. Soon God's Creation will be restored. He alone is worthy of praise. Verses 16-17:

16 **And the four and twenty elders, which sat before God on their seats, fell upon their faces, and worshipped God, 17 Saying, We give thee thanks, O Lord God Almighty, which art, and wast, and**

art to come; because thou hast taken to thee thy great power, and hast reigned.

As God reveals His righteousness and perfection, the nations become more angry. The finale has come. Those who feared God and depend upon Him shall be rewarded. Yet, others reject God. In their pride, they try to earn their own righteousness. They fight against the God Who created them. Verse 18:

> 18 And the nations were angry, and thy wrath is come, and the time of the dead, that they should be judged, and that thou shouldest give reward unto thy servants the prophets, and to the saints, and them that fear thy name, small and great; and shouldest destroy them which destroy the earth.

The Temple of God is opened. There is evidence of God's power and might. God, the LORD of hosts, now is sending His Son. Verse 19:

> 19 And the temple of God was opened in heaven, and there was seen in his temple the ark of his testament: and there were lightnings, and voices, and thunderings, and an earthquake, and great hail.

The last book in the Old Testament is Malachi. This prophet wrote the following warning to the Jews. Malachi 3:1-2:

> 1 . . . behold, he shall come, saith the LORD of hosts. 2 But who may abide the day of his coming? and who shall stand when he appeareth? for he is like a refiner's fire . . .

12

Revelation 12

We are now in what is called "the third woe" (Rev. 11:14). This is the last of three. John records what he sees. Revelation 12:1-2:

1 And there appeared a great wonder in heaven; a woman clothed with the sun, and the moon under her feet, and upon her head a crown of twelve stars: 2 And she being with child cried, travailing in birth, and pained to be delivered.

Who is this woman or who does she represent? There is a very interesting story in Genesis 37 about a dream Joseph had. Joseph was one of the twelve sons of Israel. We are told, ". . . Israel loved Joseph more than all his children . . . And when his brethren saw that their father loved him more than all his brethren, they hated him, and could not speak peaceably unto him" (Gen. 37:3-4). Joseph had two dreams and he shares the second dream with his brothers and his father Israel. Genesis 37:9-11:

> 9 And he dreamed yet another dream, and told it his brethren, and said, Behold, I have dreamed a dream more; and, behold, the sun and the moon and the eleven stars made obeisance [bowed down in reverence] to me. 10 And he told it to his father, and to his brethren: and his father rebuked him, and said unto him, What is this dream that thou hast dreamed? Shall I and thy mother and thy brethren indeed come to bow down ourselves to thee to the earth? 11 And his brethren envied him; but his father observed the saying.

This is allegorical and considered to be a "type" because it represents something that will happen in the future. Joseph will save his father Israel and his eleven brothers from death. This is in spite of the fact his brethren hate him and want to kill him out of jealousy. This sounds similar to Jesus Christ. His own people knew Him not and killed Him. This woman has a crown of twelve stars – one for each of the twelve tribes. Let us see if the text confirms this. Revelation 12:3-5:

3 And there appeared another wonder in heaven; and behold a great red dragon, having seven heads and ten horns, and seven crowns upon his heads. **4** And his tail drew the third part of the stars of heaven, and did cast them to the earth: and the dragon stood before the woman which was ready to be delivered, for to devour her child as soon as it was born.

5 And she brought forth a man child, who was to rule all nations with a rod of iron: and her child was caught up unto God, and to his throne.

I think we have our confirmation. Satan has done everything to prevent the Seed of the woman from being born. God cursed Satan because of his role in the fall of mankind, "And I will put enmity between thee and the woman, and between thy seed and her seed; it [her Seed] shall bruise thy head, and thou shalt bruise his heel" (Gen. 3:15). The Son of Man will defeat Satan who hates this man-child, Jesus Christ.

The woman represents Israel who fled into the wilderness. How long does the following verse say that God will provide for her? There is that number again. Whether it is three and one-half years, forty-two months, or one thousand two hundred and sixty days, it is all the same! In the latter half of the seven years, God will protect and provide for true Israel. Verse 6:

> 6 **And the woman fled into the wilder-ness, where she hath a place prepared of God, that they should feed her there a thousand two hundred and threescore days.**

You saw the above reference to "a great red dragon" (v. 3). We are told that "his tail drew the third part of the stars of heaven, and did cast them to the earth" (v. 4). When Lucifer rebelled against God, he took with him one-third of the heavenly beings. Since then, he has set about to subvert God's plan to restore Creation at every step. For a deeper insight into this, read Ezekiel 28. The culmination of Revelation is the final battle. Satan, formerly Lucifer, is cast out of heaven to earth along with the fallen angels who followed him. We continue with verses 7-10:

> 7 **And there was war in heaven: Michael and his angels fought against the dragon; and the dragon fought and his angels, 8 And prevailed not; neither was their place found any more in heaven. 9 And the great dragon was cast out, that old serpent, called the Devil, and Satan,**

which deceiveth the whole world: he was cast out into the earth, and his angels were cast out with him.

John hears the pronouncement made. The time has come. Satan who has been the constant Accuser of the brethren during the Tribulation will be expelled from heaven. Verse 10:

10 **And I heard a loud voice saying in heaven, Now is come salvation, and strength, and the kingdom of our God, and the power of his Christ: for the accuser of our brethren is cast down, which accused them before our God day and night.**

However, those who loved the Lamb more than their own lives have been saved by the blood of the Lamb. Verse 11:

11 **And they [the brethren] overcame him [Satan] by the blood of the Lamb, and by the word of their testimony; and they loved not their lives unto the death.**

All heaven is to rejoice. Satan and his fallen angels have now been cast out of heaven. Verse 12:

12 **Therefore rejoice, ye heavens, and ye that dwell in them. Woe to the inhabiters of the earth and of the sea! for the devil is come down unto you, having great wrath, because he knoweth that he hath but a short time.**

The "third woe" was mentioned earlier. This is the last and most terrifying because Satan and his fallen angels are cast out of heaven and loosed upon the earth. They know their time is limited. The last half of the Tribulation is called the Great Tribulation for this reason. Satan hates this woman who is Israel and seeks to destroy. If it were not for God's supernatural protection, that might have been accomplished. Verses 13-14:

13 **And when the dragon saw that he was cast unto the earth, he persecuted the woman which brought forth the man child. 14 And to the woman were given two wings of a great eagle, that she might fly into the wilderness, into her place, where she is nourished for a time, and times, and half a time, from the face of the serpent.**

This is similar to Israel's escape from the Pharoah of Egypt who also sought to destroy Israel.

Did you notice the time reference in verse 14? Let us stop for a moment as it makes sense. A time is a year, times is two years, and half a time is a half-year. God will protect and preserve the true children of Abraham during the Great Tribulation. In this time of duress, they need to continue in their faith by trusting God's Word, and endure to the end. They must depend upon God. He will do for them what He did for them in the past. Like their father Abraham, they must believe God and it will be counted to them as righteousness. (See Genesis 15:6.) Remember how the angel of death passed over them because of the blood of the Passover Lamb! Remember and believe! God will deliver them. Exodus 19:3-4:

> **3 And Moses went up unto God, and the LORD called unto him out of the mountain, saying, <u>Thus shalt thou say to the house of Jacob, and tell the children of Israel</u>; 4 Ye have seen what I did unto the Egyptians, and <u>how I bare you on eagles' wings, and brought you unto myself</u>.**

To whom are these words intended? Verse 6:

> **6 . . . These are the words which thou shalt speak unto the children of Israel.**

Satan attempts to destroy Israel by supernatural means, but God responds. Verses 15-16:

> 15 **And the serpent cast out of his mouth water as a flood after the woman, that he might cause her to be carried away of the flood.** 16 **And the earth helped the woman, and the earth opened her mouth, and swallowed up the flood which the dragon cast out of his mouth.**

Satan is very angry at true Israel who chooses to "keep the commandments of God, and have the testimony of Jesus Christ." Verse 17:

> 17 **And the dragon was wroth [very angry] with the woman, and went to make war with the remnant of her seed, which keep the commandments of God, and have the testimony of Jesus Christ.**

13

Revelation 13

The Apostle John seems to be transported to another place and there he observes a sea. He records his vision. This is allegorical and we will need to uncover its meaning. Revelations 13:1:

> 1 **And I stood upon the sand of the sea, and saw a beast rise up out of the sea, having seven heads and ten horns, and upon his horns ten crowns, and upon his heads the name of blasphemy.**

As we read this, we are puzzled. How will we be able to understand this? There is good news. We have in our possession the most powerful tool for interpreting the Bible. What is that? It is the Bible. We will let Scripture interpret Scripture. I have good news. This is not the first time these words have been written. This vision was first seen by the prophet Daniel. We will use this information to aid in our interpretation.

Earlier, I made a comparison to the book of Revelation being like a theatrical production. It has scenes and actors upon a stage. Much of what John records in these visions are not natural to this world. What do I mean? They are supernatural. We are given a glimpse into the unseen spiritual realm. There is a malevolent hierarchy that mimics God's world. It may be counterfeit, but it is real. Paul wrote, "For we wrestle not against flesh and blood, but against principalities, against powers, against the rulers of the darkness of this world, against spiritual wickedness in high places" (Eph. 6:12). The book of Daniel provides us with a glimpse into this realm. God dispatched the angel Gabriel to respond to Daniel's prayer. However, Gabriel was delayed due to a battle with the Prince of Persia. Another verse mentions the Prince of Grecia. (See Daniel 10:13, 20.) These various princes in the spiritual realm serve the Prince of the power of the air. These fallen angels, along with Satan, continue to rebel against God.

We are going to find that there is an unholy trinity which is a counterfeit of the Holy Trinity. Satan purports to be the god of this world. The Antichrist will represent Satan in the flesh. He is called the Beast. Verses 2-4:

2 And the beast which I saw was like unto a leopard, and his feet were as the feet of a bear, and his mouth as the mouth of a lion: and the dragon [Satan] gave him his power, and his seat, and great authority. 3 And I saw one of his heads as it were wounded to death; and his deadly wound was healed: and all the world wondered after the beast. 4 And they worshipped the dragon which gave power unto the beast: and they worshipped the beast, saying, Who is like unto the beast? who is able to make war with him?

This unholy trinity consists of Satan, the Antichrist, and, finally, the False Prophet. Verses 5-6:

5 And there was given unto him a mouth speaking great things and blasphemies; and power was given unto him to continue forty and two months. 6 And he opened his mouth in blasphemy against God, to blaspheme his name, and his tabernacle, and them that dwell in heaven.

Have you ever been in a skyscraper and looked down upon the streets and watched the ebb and flow of people? They look like water. It is generally understood the "sea" means "a sea of people." Out of this sea these creatures come. At this point, we need to turn to Daniel for clarification before we return to our text. God is showing Daniel there will be successive world leaders who rise up out of the "sea of people." Daniel 7:2-7:

> 2 Daniel spake and said, I saw in my vision by night, and, behold, the four winds of the heaven strove upon the great sea. 3 And four great beasts <u>came up from the sea</u>, diverse one from another.

> 4 The first was like a lion, and had eagle's wings: I beheld till the wings thereof were plucked, and it was lifted up from the earth, and made stand upon the feet as a man, and a man's heart was given to it. 5 And behold another beast, a second, like to a bear, and it raised up itself on one side, and it had three ribs in the mouth of it between the teeth of it: and they said thus unto it, Arise, devour much flesh. 6 After this I beheld, and lo another, like a leopard, which had upon the back of it four wings of a fowl; the beast had also four heads; and

dominion was given to it. 7 After this I saw in the night visions, and behold a fourth beast, dreadful and terrible, and strong exceedingly; and it had great iron teeth: it devoured and brake in pieces, and stamped the residue with the feet of it: and it was diverse [different] from all the beasts that were before it; and it had ten horns.

Next, we need to go to Daniel 2 where he interprets a dream for King Nebuchadnezzar. There is a statue with a head of gold and feet of iron and clay. Each part of this statue represents the future stages of Gentile rule beginning with Babylon and ending with Rome. The statue's parts represent a series of consecutive historic kings or governments who, as Gentile nations, serve man and not God. (For detailed analysis, see the list of Bible surveys in the back of the book.) Presently, we are in a fragmented form of Rome. Here is my point. If this is the case, and I believe it is, then the ruler to be feared the most is the last in the series who is the Antichrist. How bad is it? Daniel tells us that the government of the Antichrist is "dreadful and terrible, and strong exceedingly; and it had great iron teeth: it devoured and brake in pieces, and stamped the residue with the feet of it" (v. 7). What about these ten horns?

Horns are something that grow up out of something else such as a bull or male goat. It can represent an entity that comes out of another entity. Daniel speaks about the ten horns. Verse 8:

> 8 **I considered the horns, and, behold, there came up among them another little horn, before whom there were three of the first horns plucked up by the roots: and, behold, in this horn were eyes like the eyes of man, and a mouth speaking great things.**

This little horn is subservient to the beast whom he will serve. Now, as we return to the text. be aware that it might repeat some of the information presented in Daniel 7.

In our text, the Apostle John is talking about this beast or the Antichrist. Revelations 13:7-8:

> 7 **And it was given unto him to make war with the saints, and to overcome them: and power was given him over all kindreds, and tongues, and nations. 8 And all that dwell upon the earth shall worship him, whose names are not written in the book of life of the Lamb slain from the foundation of the world.**

The Antichrist is allowed to exercise power over all whose names are not written in the Lamb's book of life. These are the rebellious Gentiles and it includes the tribes of Israel who have no faith. John, inspired by the Spirit, gives a warning to the readers. Verses 9-10:

> **9 If any man have an ear, let him hear. 10 He that leadeth into captivity shall go into captivity: he that killeth with the sword must be killed with the sword. Here is the patience and the faith of the saints.**

The saints are those who follow the Gospel of the Kingdom. They should not lead anyone into captivity nor should they kill with the sword. Instead, they are to have patience and faith. They are to wait on God and believe His Word.

Do you remember Christ's teaching called the Beatitudes? He was teaching the children of Israel, "Blessed are the meek: for they shall inherit the earth" (Matt. 5:5). Who will inherit the earth? Those who are saved by the Gospel of the Kingdom. They are to be *meek* which means *mildly tempered, having a gentle spirit, loving their enemy, and not being easily provoked.* Christ, Israel's King, will be the victor over their enemies! He will crush them. Thus, there is no need for them to fight. By doing so, they will show their lack of faith in God's promises!

We will now be introduced to the third "beast" of the three unholy trinity: the false prophet. He is like the others before him, but his purpose is to bring everything on earth under the control of the first beast who is the Antichrist. Verses 11-12:

> 11 **And I beheld another beast coming up out of the earth; and he had two horns like a lamb, and he spake as a dragon.** 12 **And he exerciseth all the power of the first beast before him, and causeth the earth and them which dwell therein to worship the first beast, whose deadly wound was healed.**

For Israel to accept the testimony from a prophet as being credible, the prophet must be authenticated. How is he authenticated? It is by miracles, wonders, and signs. When Jesus came to confirm the promises made to the fathers (Rom. 15:8), He came in the office of a Prophet. The Messiah has three offices: Prophet, Priest, and King. During Jesus' earthly ministry, He was validated as a Prophet. Because of God's authentication by miracles, wonders, and signs, the Jews listened to Him. Now, Satan will create his own prophet and validate him by counterfeit miracles, wonders, and signs. Verses 13-14:

13 And he [the false prophet] doeth great wonders, so that he maketh fire come down from heaven on the earth in the sight of men, 14 And deceiveth them that dwell on the earth by the means of those miracles which he had power to do in the sight of the beast [Antichrist]; saying to them that dwell on the earth, that they should make an image to the beast, which had the wound by a sword, and did live.

The false prophet draws all people from the earth to worship "the image" of the beast. Notice what happens to those who refuse to worship the beast. It says that they "should be killed." Verse 15:

15 And he had power to give life unto the image of the beast, that the image of the beast should both speak, and cause that as many as would not worship the image of the beast should be killed.

Here is where "the mark" of the beast is mentioned. Everyone is required to show allegiance to the beast by taking "the mark" which is similar to ownership. Without identifying with the beast, they will be unable to buy or sell. Verses 16-17:

> 16 **And he causeth all, both small and great, rich and poor, free and bond, to receive a mark in their right hand, or in their foreheads: 17 And that no man might buy or sell, save [except] he that had the mark, or the name of the beast, or the number of his name.**

The origin of "666" as the mark of the beast is stated but not explained. There are many theories. One states that the number seven symbolizes perfection and six is the deficiency of perfection. Therefore the unholy trinity would be marked as "6 6 6." Whatever the mark is, it is more important that we understand its purpose. It is to identify those who pledge allegiance to the Antichrist. It should be avoided at all cost. For those who take the mark, there can be no salvation. Verse 18:

> 18 **Here is wisdom. Let him that hath understanding count the number of the beast: for it is the number of a man; and his number is Six hundred threescore and six.**

14

Revelation 14

John records the following event. The Messiah, the Lamb of God, is standing on Mount Zion which is spelled "Sion" below. Along with Him are one hundred forty-four thousand who are dedicated to Him. Mount Zion was initially identified as the City of David. Specifically, it refers to the Temple Mount where Abraham would have sacrificed his son Isaac. Revelation 14:1-5:

> 1 **And I looked, and, lo, <u>a Lamb stood on the mount Sion, and with him an hundred forty and four thousand,</u> having his Father's name written in their foreheads. 2 And I heard a voice from heaven, as the voice of many waters, and as the voice of a great thunder: and I heard the voice of harpers harping with their harps: 3 And they sung as it**

were a new song before the throne, and before the four beasts, and the elders: and no man could learn that song but the hundred and forty and four thousand, which were redeemed from the earth.

So that there is no confusion, the four beasts or creatures mentioned above are not the beasts who are associated with the unholy trinity.

There are one hundred forty-four thousand which surround the Lamb. They are the witnesses for the Gospel of the Kingdom and were killed by the beast because of the gospel. Now, they accompany the Lamb wherever He goes. John describes them as virtuous and faultless before God's throne. Verses 4-5:

4 These are they which were not defiled with women; for they are virgins. These are they which follow the Lamb whithersoever he goeth. These were redeemed from among men, being the firstfruits unto God and to the Lamb. 5 And in their mouth was found no guile: for they are without fault before the throne of God.

John sees another angel who carries "the everlasting gospel" which is to be preached to all nations. This is their final chance for repentance. Verse 6:

6 And I saw another angel fly in the midst of heaven, having the everlasting gospel to preach unto them that dwell on the earth, and to every nation, and kindred, and tongue, and people,

What is it that they should do to be saved? The message is simple. They are to repent of their rebellion and glorify God Who alone is worthy. Verse 7:

7 Saying with a loud voice, Fear God, and give glory to him; for the hour of his judgment is come: and worship him that made heaven, and earth, and the sea, and the fountains of waters.

A second angel makes a proclamation that Babylon the Great has fallen. Since the days of Nimrod and Astarte, this city has served as a city of wickedness. Verse 8:

8 And there followed another angel, saying, Babylon is fallen, is fallen, that great city, because she made all nations drink of the wine of the wrath of her

fornication.

Then, a third angel appears warning of the consequences of taking the mark of the beast. Verses 9-10:

> 9 **And the third angel followed them, saying with a loud voice, If any man worship the beast and his image, and receive his mark in his forehead, or in his hand, 10 The same shall drink of the wine of the wrath of God, which is poured out without mixture into the cup of his indignation; and he shall be tormented with fire and brimstone in the presence of the holy angels, and in the presence of the Lamb:**

Those who take the mark of the beast have aligned themselves with Satan, the Antichrist, and the false prophet. There is no turning back. Their destiny is sealed. Verse 11:

> 11 **And the smoke of their torment ascendeth up for ever and ever: and they have no rest day nor night, who worship the beast and his image, and whosoever receiveth the mark of his name.**

This is in stark contrast to those who "keep the

commandments of God, and the faith of Jesus." These faithful will be blessed and rest from their labors. They will enjoy the rewards of their works. Verses 12-13:

> 12 **Here is the patience of the saints: here are they that keep the commandments of God, and the faith of Jesus. 13 And I heard a voice from heaven saying unto me, Write, Blessed are the dead which die in the Lord from henceforth: Yea, saith the Spirit, that they may rest from their labours; and their works do follow them.**

Jesus is called the Son of Man as he is both the Son of Abraham and of Adam. He is fully God, but also fully man. He appears with a crown on His head and a sickle in His hand. This is the time of the harvest. Verses 14-16:

> 14 **And I looked, and behold a white cloud, and upon the cloud one sat like unto the Son of man, having on his head a golden crown, and in his hand a sharp sickle. 15 And another angel came out of the temple, crying with a loud voice to him that sat on the cloud, Thrust in thy sickle, and reap: for the time is come for**

thee to reap; for the harvest of the earth is ripe. 16 And he that sat on the cloud thrust in his sickle on the earth; and the earth was reaped.

During His earthly ministry, Jesus told Israel that there would be harvest and judgment to come. Now, that day of the Lord has come. Joel 3:13-16:

13 Put ye in the sickle, for the harvest is ripe: come, get you down; for the press is full, the fats overflow; for their wickedness is great. 14 Multitudes, multitudes in the valley of decision: for the day of the LORD is near in the valley of decision. 15 The sun and the moon shall be darkened, and the stars shall withdraw their shining. 16 The LORD also shall roar out of Zion, and utter his voice from Jerusalem; and the heavens and the earth shall shake: but the LORD will be the hope of his people, and the strength of the children of Israel.

Jesus was asked by His disciples if they should separate the tares which is weeds from the wheat. He responded, "Let both grow together until the harvest: and in the time of harvest I will say to the reapers, Gather ye together first the tares, and bind them

them in bundles to burn them: but gather the wheat into my barn" (Matt. 13:30). Now, this is the time of the harvest. The reapers are ready to begin. Verse 17:

> 17 **And another angel came out of the temple which is in heaven, he also having a sharp sickle.**

The above has to do with the Gentiles. However, those who are Jews are treated differently by God because of their father Abraham. Before we continue, we will look at a parable told by Jesus.

The parable is found in the Gospel of Luke. It has to do with the religious leaders who were given authority over the nation of Israel. Luke 20:9-18:

> 9 **Then began he to speak to the people this parable; A certain man planted a vineyard, and let it forth to husbandmen, and went into a far country for a long time. 10 And at the season he sent a servant to the husbandmen, that they should give him of the fruit of the vineyard: but the husbandmen beat him, and sent him away empty.**
>
> 11 **And again he sent another servant: and they beat him also, and entreated**

him shamefully, and sent him away empty. 12 And again he sent a third: and they wounded him also, and cast him out. 13 Then said the lord of the vineyard, What shall I do? I will send my beloved son: it may be they will reverence him when they see him. 14 But when the husbandmen saw him, they reasoned among themselves, saying, This is the heir: come, let us kill him, that the inheritance may be ours. 15 So they cast him out of the vineyard, and killed him. What therefore shall the lord of the vineyard do unto them?

16 He shall come and destroy these husbandmen, and shall give the vineyard to others. And when they heard it, they said, God forbid. 17 And he beheld them, and said, What is this then that is written, The stone which the builders rejected, the same is become the head of the corner? 18 Whosoever shall fall upon that stone shall be broken; but on whomsoever it shall fall, it will grind him to powder.

God sent prophets to Israel, but they killed them. Finally, He sent His Son, and they killed Him too.

As we return to our text, John changes the allegory from wheat and tares to grapes and a vineyard. Verses 18-19:

> 18 And another angel came out from the altar, which had power over fire; and cried with a loud cry to him that had the sharp sickle, saying, Thrust in thy sharp sickle, and gather the clusters of the vine of the earth; for her grapes are fully ripe. 19 And the angel thrust in his sickle into the earth, and gathered the vine of the earth, and cast it into the great winepress of the wrath of God.

The winepress represents squeezing the goodness out of the grapes. Time after time, God has shown patience, kindness, and mercy towards Israel. He has stored up His wrath until this day. Isaiah 63:3-4:

> 3 I have trodden the winepress alone; and of the people there was none with me: for I will tread them in mine anger, and trample them in my fury; and their blood shall be sprinkled upon my garments, and I will stain all my raiment.
>
> 4 For the day of vengeance is in mine

heart, and the year of my redeemed is come.

This is the winepress about which the Apostle John is now speaking. The winepress is located outside the city of Jerusalem. We are told the depth at the winepress and how far the blood traveled. It was about five feet at its deepest spot. Since a furlong is about six hundred sixty feet, I estimated that it flowed as far as two hundred miles. Verse 20:

> 20 **And the winepress was trodden without the city, and blood came out of the winepress, even unto the horse bridles, by the space of a thousand and six hundred furlongs.**

15

Revelation 15

The previous chapter discussed the wrath of God. Many are used to hearing about God's mercy and love. It may seem out of character for God to exact vengeance upon His enemies. The time for mercy and love has run out like the sand in an hour glass.

I would like to take you back to the very beginning of Jesus' earthly ministry. Jesus was baptized by John the Baptist. After forty days of testing in the wilderness, He returned and entered a synagogue. Asked to read from Scripture, He read from the prophet Isaiah. He stopped before the word "and." Giving the scroll to the attendant, He went to sit down. All eyes were upon Him because He stopped mid-verse. He made a proclamation that, in their hearing, the first portion of the Scripture was fulfilled. (See Luke 4:16-20.)

This is another example of the word "and" being used for two consecutive but not concurrent events. Here is the part He read. Isaiah 61:1-2:

> 1 **The Spirit of the Lord GOD is upon me; because the LORD hath anointed me to preach good tidings unto the meek; he hath sent me to bind up the brokenhearted, to proclaim liberty to the captives, and the opening of the prison to them that are bound;**
>
> 2 **To proclaim the acceptable year of the LORD . . .**

We will see that the last verse is truncated. In other words, Jesus stopped mid-verse. In the presence of all the Jews attending, He proclaimed that this prophecy was fulfilled in their hearing. The remainder of the verse was not fulfilled then, but it is now! Here is the remainder of verse 2:

> 2 **. . . and the day of vengeance of our God; to comfort all that mourn;**

Mankind, in their conscience, is aware of the coming Judgment. Now "is" the day of vengeance of our God. Additionally, He promises to comfort true Israel. Revelation 15:1:

1 And I saw another sign in heaven, great and marvellous, seven angels having the seven last plagues; for in them is filled up <u>the wrath of God</u>.

The visions that John saw must have been surreal. Here, he sees people who are standing on a glassy sea with flames of fire. Verses 2-4:

2 And I saw as it were a sea of glass mingled with fire: and them that had gotten the victory over the beast, and over his image, and over his mark, and over the number of his name, stand on the sea of glass, having the harps of God.

3 And they sing the song of Moses the servant of God, and the song of the Lamb, saying, Great and marvellous are thy works, Lord God Almighty; just and true are thy ways, thou King of saints.

4 Who shall not fear thee, O Lord, and glorify thy name? for thou only art holy: for all nations shall come and worship before thee; for thy judgments are made manifest [known].

In the following, it mentions the "the tabernacle of the testimony." The Tabernacle of the Testimony is also called the Tabernacle of Witness. It is a tent-like structure used by the children of Israel during their sojourn in the Wilderness. Moses had it constructed according to God's specific instructions. It housed the Ark of the Covenant. This Ark held the tablets of the Ten Commandments which are referred to as "the testimony." Verses 5-6:

> 5 **And after that I looked, and, behold, the temple of the tabernacle of the testimony in heaven was opened: 6 And the seven angels came out of the temple, having the seven plagues, clothed in pure and white linen, and having their breasts girded with golden girdles.**

Remember, angels are dispatched by God as messengers. These seven angels will each deliver messages of judgment held within golden vials filled with "the wrath of God." Verse 7:

> 7 **And one of the four beasts gave unto the seven angels seven golden vials full of the wrath of God, who liveth for ever and ever.**

I picture the temple being like a furnace burning with God's anger so that smoke billowed out and no one

124

could enter. Verse 8:

> **8 And the temple was filled with smoke from the glory of God, and from his power; and no man was able to enter into the temple, till the seven plagues of the seven angels were fulfilled.**

In the next chapter, we will learn about "the plagues of the seven angels."

16

Revelation 16

In the previous chapter, we saw that God was in His temple which was filled with fire and smoke. John records His words as He spoke them from within the temple. Revelation 16:1:

> 1 And I heard a great voice out of the temple saying to the seven angels, Go your ways, and pour out the vials of the wrath of God upon the earth.

Each of the seven angels had one of the "seven golden vials full of the wrath of God" (Rev. 15:7). Verse 2:

> 2 And the first went, and poured out his vial upon the earth; and there fell a noisome and grievous sore upon the men which had the mark of the beast, and

upon them which worshipped his image.

In succession, each angel proceeds to dispense the content of their vial. The first causes repulsive and serious sores upon the bodies of the rebellious. The second turns the water of the sea into "the blood of a dead man" causing marine life to die. Verse 3:

3 **And the second angel poured out his vial upon the sea; and it became as the blood of a dead man: and every living soul died in the sea.**

In retaliation for spilling "the blood of saints and prophets," God causes the sources of drinking water to be turned to blood also. Verses 4-6:

4 **And the third angel poured out his vial upon the rivers and fountains of waters; and they became blood. 5 And I heard the angel of the waters say, Thou art righteous, O Lord, which art, and wast, and shalt be, because thou hast judged thus. 6 For they have shed the blood of saints and prophets, and thou hast given them blood to drink; for they are worthy.**

You may recall those who were "under the altar the souls of them that were slain for the word of God, and for the testimony which they held" (Rev. 6:9). A voice from these martyrs speaks out from under the altar and the words justify God's actions. Verse 7:

> 7 And I heard another out of the altar say, Even so, Lord God Almighty, true and righteous are thy judgments.

Every judgment is justified. They are intended to punish and motivate the rebellious to repent, but they do not. Verses 8-9:

> 8 And the fourth angel poured out his vial upon the sun; and power was given unto him to scorch men with fire. 9 And men were scorched with great heat, and blasphemed the name of God, which hath power over these plagues: and they repented not to give him glory.

The fourth increases the intensity of the sun's heat to burn. Instead of repentance, they blasphemed God's name. The same happens with the fifth vial. It is directed at "the seat of the beast" who is the Antichrist "and his kingdom." Verses 10-11:

> 10 And the fifth angel poured out his

vial upon the seat of the beast; and his kingdom was full of darkness; and they gnawed their tongues for pain, 11 And blasphemed the God of heaven because of their pains and their sores, and repented not of their deeds.

Only two of the seven vials remain. God's punishment is both justified and necessary. It is retribution for breaking God's Moral Law. It is intended to bring the perpetrators to repentance. With the water of the Euphrates evaporating, we are told there is a reason. It is to prepare "the way of the kings of the east." Armies will soon gather together to fight against the Holy One. This will prepare the way for the armies in the east to move their troops. Verse 12:

12 And the sixth angel poured out his vial upon the great river Euphrates; and the water thereof was dried up, that the way of the kings of the east might be prepared.

In response, something supernatural occurs. Out of the unholy trinity, "unclean spirits" issue from their mouths. I believe these are demons who serve them. Notice their effect upon "the kings of the earth and of the whole world." They mobilize the nations against God and His holy people. Verses 13-14:

13 And I saw three unclean spirits like frogs come out of the mouth of the dragon, and out of the mouth of the beast, and out of the mouth of the false prophet. 14 For they are the spirits of devils, working miracles, which go forth unto the kings of the earth and of the whole world, to gather them to the battle of that great day of God Almighty.

While Jesus was on earth and walking among His own, He taught them to watch and be ready. Matthew 24:42-44:

42 Watch therefore: for ye know not what hour your Lord doth come. 43 But know this, that if the goodman of the house had known in what watch the thief would come, he would have watched, and would not have suffered his house to be broken up. 44 <u>Therefore be ye also ready: for in such an hour as ye think not the Son of man cometh.</u>

We return to our text. Revelation 16:15-16:

15 Behold, I come as a thief. Blessed is he that watcheth, and keepeth his gar-

**ments, lest he walk naked, and they see
his shame. 16 And he gathered them together into a place called in the Hebrew
tongue Armageddon.**

Armageddon is a plain located eight miles north of
Jerusalem. It encompasses an area of two hundred
twenty-five square miles. The kings of the earth will
be gathered there as they await the offensive to destroy Jerusalem.

When Jesus was upon the Cross, His final
words were, "It is finished." (See John 19:30.) He accomplished the will of the Father and became the
propitiation for the sins of mankind. Through Him,
salvation could be offered. Those who rejected God's
offers of salvation and continued to rebel against
Him must, according to righteousness, face the consequences of their sins. His plan to redeem mankind
and restore Creation is almost finished. With the
pouring out of the seventh vial, judgment will be
complete. Likewise, God will finally say, "It is done!"
Verse 17:

**17 And the seventh angel poured out his
vial into the air; and there came a great
voice out of the temple of heaven, from
the throne, saying, It is done.**

The effects are felt globally. There is an earthquake of epic proportion as one never seen before. Here are its effects. Verses 18-20:

> 18 And there were voices, and thunders, and lightnings; and there was a great earthquake, such as was not since men were upon the earth, so mighty an earthquake, and so great. 19 And the great city was divided into three parts, and the cities of the nations fell: and great Babylon came in remembrance before God, to give unto her the cup of the wine of the fierceness of his wrath. 20 And every island fled away, and the mountains were not found.

God causes enormous hail to fall from heaven. Most historians estimate the weight of a Hebrew talent to be seventy-five pounds. The hail is like stones falling from heaven. The response of the unrepentant is to blaspheme against God. Verse 21:

> 21 And there fell upon men a great hail out of heaven, every stone about the weight of a talent: and men blasphemed God because of the plague of the hail; for the plague thereof was exceeding great.

17

Revelation 17

The angel who carried the seventh golden vial desires to show something to the Apostle John. Revelation 17:1-2:

> 1 **And there came one of the seven angels which had the seven vials, and talked with me, saying unto me, Come hither; I will shew unto thee the judgment of the great whore that sitteth upon many waters:** 2 **With whom the kings of the earth have committed fornication, and the inhabitants of the earth have been made drunk with the wine of her fornication.**

The following is an allegory. First we will read it and then unpack it. Verses 3-6:

3 So he carried me away in the spirit into the wilderness: and I saw a woman sit upon a scarlet coloured beast, full of names of blasphemy, having seven heads and ten horns. **4** And the woman was arrayed in purple and scarlet colour, and decked with gold and precious stones and pearls, having a golden cup in her hand full of abominations and filthiness of her fornication: **5** And upon her forehead was a name written, MYSTERY, BABYLON THE GREAT, THE MOTHER OF HARLOTS AND ABOMINATIONS OF THE EARTH. **6** And I saw the woman drunken with the blood of the saints, and with the blood of the martyrs of Jesus: and when I saw her, I wondered with great admiration.

What!?! John's response is surprising. That is until you realize the power of seduction held by this woman. She is the great Babylon. Many have fallen prey to her wiles which are clever and deceitful. Her power is seduction which she uses to manipulate or persuade. Her enticements lure the unsuspecting. Even John seems to have fallen prey to her persuasion. She is evil.

The angel rebukes John and reveals to him who

this woman is and her connection to the beast upon whom she rides. He is the Antichrist. Verses 7-8:

> 7 **And the angel said unto me, Wherefore didst thou marvel? I will tell thee the mystery of the woman, and of the beast that carrieth her, which hath the seven heads and ten horns. 8 The beast that thou sawest was, and is not; and shall ascend out of the bottomless pit, and go into perdition: and they that dwell on the earth shall wonder, whose names were not written in the book of life from the foundation of the world, when they behold <u>the beast that was, and is not, and yet is.</u>**

We will pause for a moment as there are questions that need to be answered. Before I answer these questions, I would like to recommend two books for your consideration. The first is *The Two Babylons* written by Alexander Hislop with the most recent edition published in 1903. It presents an argument that the Roman Catholic Church is connected to ancient Babylon. The second book is *Earth's Earliest Ages* by G. H. Pember. It was written in 1876 and updated in 1911. He argues that there was a creation before Adam and provides biblical evidence to support his conclusion. This explains Satan's claim over the earth and the origin of demons. In my opinion, both of these books are worth your time to read. I enjoy teaching the Bible and watching people "get it." I live for that. The challenge is trying not to provide too much information. For an overall understanding of God's plan and purpose, I recommend Bible students read a theological survey. It provides for a solid foundational understanding. A good expositional sermon or commentary gives you a personal per-spective or opinion. You may agree with them or not, but you should be able to give your reasons why. It is a mark of someone who is "strong" in the faith.

There are still questions from the above verses that need to be answered. Who is this woman? What is her connection to the beast? Also, what does John mean by "the beast that was, and is not, and yet is?" Let us go back to the time of Noah. Every human is a direct descendant of Adam and Noah through his three sons. Following the Flood, God instructed Noah and his sons, ". . . Be fruitful, and multiply, and replenish the earth" (Gen. 9:1). This is in the King James translation. The word *replenish* means to *refill* and implies that something was once full and needs to be filled again. There are two places in which the word *replenish* is used: God's instructions to Noah (Gen. 1:28) and God's instructions to Adam and Eve (Gen. 9:1). The latter is interesting, but not presently relevant.

Genesis 10 provides the list of Noah's offspring which will lead us to our target. One of Noah's three sons gave birth to a son named Cush. Our man of interest is Cush's son Nimrod. Genesis 10:8-10:

> **8 And Cush begat Nimrod: he began to be a mighty one in the earth. 9 He was a mighty hunter before the LORD: wherefore it is said, Even as Nimrod the mighty hunter before the LORD. 10 And <u>the beginning of his kingdom was Babel</u> . . .**

Babel was the forerunner of Babylon and Nimrod was its king. So the founder of Babel was Noah's great grandson. In his book *The Two Babylons*, Alexander Hislop presents extrabiblical evidence that Nimrod married a prostitute. Her name was Semiramis. She has other names such as Ishtar or Astarte which is the origin of the word Easter.

Nimrod was a very evil king. He, along with his queen, dominated the region. His uncle Shem was irate that he had abandoned God the Creator and served other gods. So, Shem killed Nimrod with the sword and sent his parts to the four corners of his kingdom. This was a warning to others not to forsake the God of Creation. Following Nimrod's death, his wife Astarte who was his queen claimed that Nimrod was a god. It was he who impregnated her and she had a son. He was the child-god who was named Tammuz or Bacchus who was also divine. Can you think of a similar story? Hislop provides evidence that this saga was replicated several times: first in Egypt, then in Greece, and finally in Rome. This has nothing to do with the virgin Mary, the humble mother of Jesus. Instead, it is Satan's counterfeit to a divine son. In each saga, the divine husband of the queen is killed and his widow bears a child after his death. Each saga purports that the son was divinely conceived by a god which makes the child a son of a god. In each account, the mother of the "god-child" is referred to as the Queen of the Universe. This is the woman, the prostitute who married Nimrod, who is the "MYSTERY." She is from the beginning from "BABYLON THE GREAT." She is the one who is "THE MOTHER OF HARLOTS AND ABOMINATIONS OF THE EARTH."

There are two questions that remain unanswered. What is the woman's connection to the beast? We want to understand what is meant by "that was, and is not, and yet is." Nimrod was committed to astrology. He worships the stars of which some are said to be fallen angels of the heavenly host.

The Tower of Babel was built for this, "And they said, Go to, let us build us a city and a tower, whose top may reach unto heaven; and let us make us a name . . ." (Gen. 11:4). Nimrod was an evil man and served Satan from the beginning. We are told the first beast is the Antichrist who is "the beast that was, and is not, and yet is" (v. 8). This is accomplished when Satan raised Nimrod from the dead. Then, what is the woman's relationship to the beast? I believe that it is Astarte, the Queen of Heaven. In life she was his wife. I would like to recommend another book. It is *The Return Of The Gods* by Jonathan Cahn. He is a Messianic Rabbi and presents an interesting perspective on the Old Testament. There is only God and there are no others. However, the prince of imposters created a plethora of false gods of whom he, Satan, is the prince.

Before we return to our text I would like to make something clear. Extrabiblical data obtained from archaeological finds may be historical and support the biblical narrative, but they are neither inspired nor authoritative. Depending on their authenticity, they may provide information for us to ponder, but that is the extent of it. When we read it, we must see it from that perspective.

We will now return to Revelation 17:9-11:

9 And here is the mind which hath wisdom. The seven heads are seven mountains, on which the woman sitteth. 10 And there are seven kings: five are fallen, and one is, and the other is not yet come; and when he cometh, he must continue a short space. 11 And the beast that was, and is not, even he is the eighth, and is of the seven, and goeth into perdition.

The Bible uses allegory to describe difficult concepts and those that God wishes to remain somewhat hidden. Mountains are often used to represent kingdoms as we will see in a moment. The reason for this is that ancient capitals were placed upon the tops of mountains. The city of Jerusalem was built atop a mountain. This was done for defense. Therefore, the physical locations of these capital built upon mountains represent the kingdom that ruled from them. To be consistent with Daniel's prophecy about the Gentile governments who generally opposed God are represented by a statue. (See Daniel 2.) This statue, comprised of different parts of one body, represents successive Gentile empires who would dominate the world. In the end, Jesus Christ will crush these Gentile kingdoms.

All of this concerns a dream of King Nebuchadnezzar. The prophet Daniel had to first tell the king what his dream was and, then, he could interpret it for him. Daniel makes it clear to the king that the God of Israel gave him the interpretation. It is important enough for us to include it. Daniel 2:31-35:

> 31 **Thou, O king, sawest, and behold a great image. This great image, whose brightness was excellent, stood before thee; and the form thereof was terrible. 32 This image's head was of fine <u>gold</u>, his breast and his arms of <u>silver</u>, his belly and his thighs of <u>brass</u>, 33 His legs of <u>iron</u>, his feet <u>part of iron and part of clay</u>.**
>
> 34 **Thou sawest till that <u>a stone was cut out without hands</u>, which smote the image upon his feet that were of iron and clay, and brake them to pieces. 35 Then was the iron, the clay, the brass, the silver, and the gold, broken to pieces together, and became like the chaff of the summer threshing-floors; and the wind carried them away, that no place was found for them: <u>and the stone that smote the image became a great mountain, and filled the whole earth</u>.**

The book of Daniel is a key to understanding Revelation. The stone mentioned above is Jesus Christ. He is the Stone "cut out without hands." And, what shall this Stone do? It shall strike or "smote the image upon his feet that were of iron and clay." What is the final result? He shall "brake them to pieces." Who? He will break to dust these world governments represented by this statue. Of this King and Kingdom, what shall be the final result? "The stone that smote the image became a great mountain, and filled the whole earth." This great and final kingdom is represented by "a great mountain." Daniel began by telling the king the content of what he had dreamed. Then, beginning with King Nebuchadnezzar, he explains to the king the statue represents successive kingdoms that rise and fall. You can read Daniel 2:36-45. For a detailed explanation, consider our biblical surveys. In summary, this statue represents successive kingdoms that dominate the world. The final one is Rome which still exists today as a form of global government. The destruction of this statue establishes the final supremacy of Christ's Kingdom.

As we return to our text, I want you to keep something in mind. The word "king" may denote world leaders who rule and have power over their people. Also, Daniel lived about twenty-five hundred years ago and his prophecy is nearing its fulfillment. Revelation 17:12-13:

> **12 And the ten horns which thou sawest are ten kings, which have received no kingdom as yet; but receive power as kings one hour with the beast. 13 These have one mind, and shall give their power and strength unto the beast.**

These rulers over the people were of one mind and, agreeing with the beast who is the Antichrist, they gave over their support to him. What is it that they are agreeing to do?

They will make war against the Lamb and Israel to annihilate them. However, we are told what the result will be. Verse 14:

> **14 These shall make war with the Lamb, and the Lamb shall overcome them: for he is Lord of lords, and King of kings: and they that are with him are called, and chosen, and faithful.**

When things go wrong for them, they look for someone to blame. In the final world government, it controls two divisions: government and religion. Government is headed by a man called the Antichrist.

Religion is headed by a woman called the Queen of the Universe. Due to the nature of her worship, she is referred to as "the whore." Verses 15-16:

> 15 **And he saith unto me, The waters which thou sawest, where the whore sitteth, are peoples, and multitudes, and nations, and tongues. 16 And the ten horns which thou sawest upon the beast, these shall hate the whore, and shall make her desolate and naked, and shall eat her flesh, and burn her with fire.**

Everything is going according to God's timeline. The lesser rulers have given their political power to the beast, the Antichrist. There is no need for the goddess anyways. The Antichrist is consolidating his power and will soon proclaim himself to be god! Verses 17-18:

> 17 **For God hath put in their hearts to fulfil his will, and to agree, and give their kingdom unto the beast, until the words of God shall be fulfilled. 18 And the woman which thou sawest is that great city, which reigneth over the kings of the earth.**

18

Revelation 18

Babylon is much more than a physical city. It is representative of everything against God since it was founded by Nimrod. Consider her name. "And upon her forehead was a name written, MYSTERY, BABYLON THE GREAT, THE MOTHER OF HARLOTS AND ABOMINATIONS OF THE EARTH" (Rev. 17:5). She is the epitome of sin. She is pervasive within human culture. She is the mother of harlots and abominations which are furthered by her religion.

An announcement is made of her demise. How will it affects the present world. Verses 1-3:

> 1 **And after these things I saw another angel come down from heaven, having great power; and the earth was lightened with his glory. 2 And he cried**

mightily with a strong voice, saying, <u>Babylon the great is fallen</u>, is fallen, and is become the habitation of devils, and the hold of every foul spirit, and a cage of every unclean and hateful bird. 3 For all nations have drunk of the wine of the wrath of her fornication, and the kings of the earth have committed fornication with her, and the merchants of the earth are waxed [grown] rich through the abundance of her delicacies.

It is evident that Babylon is the source of sin including avarice and greed. The statement that it has fallen is that it has lost her power because their Queen has been removed. The Antichrist will quickly take the glory given to her.

God calls His people to come out from her. This is much the same way that Grace Believers were told to come out of the world and be detached from it. James wrote to Kingdom Believers, ". . . know ye not that the friendship of the world is enmity with God? whosoever therefore will be a friend of the world is the enemy of God" (Jas. 4:4). The following is a proclamation to all who believe the Kingdom Gospel. Verses 4-5:

148

4 And I heard another voice from heaven, saying, Come out of her, my people, that ye be not partakers of her sins, and that ye receive not of her plagues. 5 For her sins have reached unto heaven, and God hath remembered her iniquities.

God will repay her wickedness. Verses 6-7:

6 Reward her even as she rewarded you, and double unto her double according to her works: in the cup which she hath filled fill to her double. 7 How much she hath glorified herself, and lived deliciously, so much torment and sorrow give her: for she saith in her heart, I sit a queen, and am no widow, and shall see no sorrow.

Notice the words from the Queen of Heaven. She is no longer the widow of Nimrod or any other. She has taken to herself many man who are kings and women also as her possession. She is the goddess who they worship and serve. Her wickedness must come to an end! Her judgment is swift. Verse 8:

8 Therefore shall her plagues come in one day, death, and mourning, and fam-

ine; and she shall be utterly burned with fire: for strong is the Lord God who judgeth her.

Here is a summary about the impact upon those who believe she was divine. Their income and livelihood depended upon her. It reminds me of Paul who told about this same goddess, then called Diana of Ephesus. The merchants were angry at Paul because he had affected their trade of silver charms and amulets. Think about the gold and silver beads, metals, statues, medallions, charms, and amulets sold today. Verses 9-19:

9 And the kings of the earth, who have committed fornication and lived deliciously with her, shall bewail her, and lament for her, when they shall see the smoke of her burning, 10 Standing afar off for the fear of her torment, saying, Alas, alas, that great city Babylon, that mighty city! for in one hour is thy judgment come. 11 And the merchants of the earth shall weep and mourn over her; for no man buyeth their merchandise any more: 12 The merchandise of gold, and silver, and precious stones, and of pearls, and fine linen, and purple, and silk, and scarlet, and all thyine wood,

and all manner vessels of ivory, and all manner vessels of most precious wood, and of brass, and iron, and marble, 13 And cinnamon, and odours, and ointments, and frankincense, and wine, and oil, and fine flour, and wheat, and beasts, and sheep, and horses, and chariots, and slaves, and souls of men.

14 And the fruits that thy soul lusted after are departed from thee, and all things which were dainty and goodly are departed from thee, and thou shalt find them no more at all. 15 The merchants of these things, which were made rich by her, shall stand afar off for the fear of her torment, weeping and wailing, 16 And saying, Alas, alas, that great city, that was clothed in fine linen, and purple, and scarlet, and decked with gold, and precious stones, and pearls!

17 For in one hour so great riches is come to nought. And every shipmaster, and all the company in ships, and sailors, and as many as trade by sea, stood afar off, 18 And cried when they saw the smoke of her burning, saying, What city

is like unto this great city?

19 And they cast dust on their heads, and cried, weeping and wailing, saying, Alas, alas, that great city, wherein were made rich all that had ships in the sea by reason of her costliness! for in one hour is she made desolate.

The world and her devotees mourn her passing and how it affects their lives. Heaven and those who follow God are told to rejoice. God has delivered retribution upon this goddess of evil. Verses 20-22:

20 Rejoice over her, thou heaven, and ye holy apostles and prophets; for God hath avenged you on her. 21 And a mighty angel took up a stone like a great millstone, and cast it into the sea, saying, Thus with violence shall that great city Babylon be thrown down, and shall be found no more at all. 22 And the voice of harpers, and musicians, and of pipers, and trumpeters, shall be heard no more at all in thee; and no craftsman, of whatsoever craft he be, shall be found any more in thee; and the sound of a millstone shall be heard no more at all in thee;

She is desolate and within her there shall only be darkness. Not even the light of one candle will shine. Neither will there be joy or gladness. Her treachery is revealed and her punishment is everlasting. Verses 23-24:

> 23 And the light of a candle shall shine no more at all in thee; and the voice of the bridegroom and of the bride shall be heard no more at all in thee: for thy merchants were the great men of the earth; for by thy sorceries were all nations deceived. 24 And in her was found the blood of prophets, and of saints, and of all that were slain upon the earth.

19

Revelation 19

The Apostle John listens to the many who are in heaven praising God. Paul said, "We are confident, I say, and willing rather to be absent from the body, and to be present with the Lord" (2 Cor. 5:8). Again, speaking to those saved by grace about the Rapture, he wrote, "Then we which are alive and remain shall be caught up together with them in the clouds, to meet the Lord in the air: and so shall we ever be with the Lord" (1 Thes. 4:17). There are many witnesses in heaven who wholeheartedly praise and cheer on God. They are watching as He redeems mankind and restores His Creation. Revelation 18:1-3:

> 1 **And after these things I heard a great voice of much people in heaven, saying, Alleluia; Salvation, and glory, and honour, and power, unto the Lord our God:**

2 For true and righteous are his judgments: for he hath judged the great whore, which did corrupt the earth with her fornication, and hath avenged the blood of his servants at her hand. 3 And again they said, Alleluia. And her smoke rose up for ever and ever.

The last vestiges of Babylon the Great are consumed by fire. Smoke rises up from her ashes. This is God's ultimate victory over the goddess.

Praises come from the twelve apostles and the twelve patriarchs who rule over the twelve tribes. The four heavenly beasts also praise Him. A voice calls out for all His servants, both great and small, to praise God! Verses 4-5:

4 And the four and twenty elders and the four beasts fell down and worshipped God that sat on the throne, saying, Amen; Alleluia. 5 And a voice came out of the throne, saying, <u>Praise our God</u>, all ye his servants, and ye that fear him, both small and great.

The praises resound and are echoed back by all Creation. Verse 6:

6 And I heard as it were the voice of a great multitude, and as the voice of many waters, and as the voice of mighty thunderings, saying, Alleluia: for the Lord God omnipotent reigneth.

Amid this jubilant praise, the voice makes an announcement concerning the Lamb and His bride. Verses 7-8:

7 Let us be glad and rejoice, and give honour to him: for the marriage of the Lamb is come, and his wife hath made herself ready. 8 And to her was granted that she should be arrayed in fine linen, clean and white: for the fine linen is the righteousness of saints.

In the Gospel of Matthew, Jesus told a parable. Matthew 22:1-2:

1 And Jesus answered and spake unto them again by parables, and said, 2 The kingdom of heaven is like unto a certain king, which made a marriage for his son,

He continues with verse 8:

157

8 Then saith he to his servants, The wedding is ready, but they which were bidden [invited] were not worthy.

Think of the children of Abraham being the invited guests for the marriage feast of the Lamb and His bride. This parable was prophetic. We continues with verses 11-13:

11 And when the king came in to see the guests, he saw there a man which had not on a wedding garment: 12 And he saith unto him, Friend, how camest thou in hither not having a wedding garment? And he was speechless. 13 Then said the king to the servants, Bind him hand and foot, and take him away, and cast him into outer darkness; there shall be weeping and gnashing of teeth.

Consider all the people who attend synagogues and churches to gain the right perspective. Verse 14:

14 For many are called, but few are chosen.

There is a wedding, but we still do not know who the bride will be. We will find out shortly. Revelation 19:9-10:

9 And he saith unto me, Write, Blessed are they which are called unto the marriage supper of the Lamb. And he saith unto me, These are the true sayings of God. 10 And I fell at his feet to worship him. And he said unto me, See thou do it not: I am thy fellowservant, and of thy brethren that have the testimony of Jesus: worship God: for the testimony of Jesus is the spirit of prophecy.

Overwhelmed, the Apostle John falls at the feet of the angel and worships him. Unlike Lucifer, who gathered the praises unto himself, this angel rejects John's praise. He tells John that he is a fellowservant and all worship is due to God alone.

In chapter 13, I wrote, "The Messiah has three offices: Prophet, Priest, and King." Here is an explanation. First, when Jesus came to confirm the promises made to the fathers, He did not speak His Own words. Instead, He spoke the words given to Him by the Father. "For I have not spoken of myself; but the Father which sent me, he gave me a commandment, what I should say, and what I should speak" (Jn. 12:49). This is the role of a Prophet. In heaven, Jesus intercedes for His people. This does not apply to those saved by the Gospel of Grace since they received the righteousness of Christ upon their salvation. This applies to those who are saved by the Gospel of the Kingdom. Upon His resurrection, God made Jesus a Priest from the order of Melchisedec. "Wherefore he is able also to save them to the uttermost that come unto God by him, seeing he ever liveth to make intercession for them" (Heb. 7:25). Jesus is interceding for true Israel as their Priest. This leaves us with His final office as King.

The last office of the Messiah is the King. He is the One Who will defend and save His people Israel. Verses 11-16:

> 11 **And I saw heaven opened, and behold a white horse; and he that sat upon him was called Faithful and True, and in righteousness he doth judge and make war. 12 His eyes were as a flame of fire, and on his head were many crowns; and he had a name written, that no man knew, but he himself. 13 And he was clothed with a vesture dipped in blood: and his name is called The Word of God. 14 And the armies which were in heaven followed him upon white horses, clothed in fine linen, white and clean. 15 And out of his mouth goeth a sharp sword, that with it he should smite the nations: and he shall rule**

them with a rod of iron: and he treadeth the winepress of the fierceness and wrath of Almighty God.

16 And he hath on his vesture and on his thigh a name written, KING OF KINGS, AND LORD OF LORDS.

In his gospel, John called Jesus the Word of God in the opening of his gospel. "In the beginning was the Word, and the Word was with God, and the Word was God" (Jn. 1:1).

There is going to be a great confrontation between good and evil. The King of Kings has arrived and is ready for the battle. There will be a lot of people killed so that the sea of blood reaches the bridle of horses. An angel invites the carnivorous fowls of heaven to a great feast. Soon, they will feed on the flesh of the fallen. Verses 17-18:

17 And I saw an angel standing in the sun; and he cried with a loud voice, saying to all the fowls that fly in the midst of heaven, Come and gather yourselves together unto the supper of the great God; 18 That ye may eat the flesh of kings, and the flesh of captains, and the flesh of mighty men, and the flesh of

horses, and of them that sit on them, and the flesh of all men, both free and bond, both small and great.

We find the following to be reminiscent of the Tower of Babel. All the people of the earth had gathered together to build a tower into heaven. God thwarted their goal of forming unity against God by changing their language and scattering them. This was the beginning of the nations. Once again, the nations do gather together again. This time they are under the Antichrist to come against God and destroy His people Israel. Verses 19-21:

19 And I saw the beast [Antichrist], and the kings of the earth, and their armies, gathered together to make war against him that sat on the horse, and against his army. 20 And the beast was taken, and with him the false prophet that wrought miracles before him, with which he deceived them that had received the mark of the beast, and them that worshipped his image. These both were cast alive into a lake of fire burning with brimstone. 21 And the remnant were slain with the sword of him that sat upon the horse, which sword proceeded out of his mouth: and all the

fowls were filled with their flesh.

There is something very important that I want you to see. Israel is not fighting! So, if Israel is not fighting this battle against evil, then Who is? It is the Lord Jesus Christ Who is KING OF KINGS, AND LORD OF LORDS. In the Beatitudes, Jesus told them that "Blessed are the meek: for they shall inherit the earth" (Matt. 5:5). Earlier, we looked at the meaning of the word *meek*. It means *mildly tempered, having a gentle spirit, loving their enemy, and not being easily provoked.* Do heirs work to earn their inheritance? No. An inheritance is a gift.

Therefore, be meek and filled with faith! This is like the day of Israel's departure from the slavery of the Egyptian Pharoah. Likewise, God will deliver His people Israel. The Antichrist is like Pharoah. The army of the Antichrist is like that of Pharoah's army. They both have the same goal. They seek to destroy Israel! Now, stop for a moment. Listen again to the words of Moses to the people. Exodus 14:13-14:

> 13 **And Moses said unto the people, <u>Fear ye not, stand still, and see the salvation of the LORD</u> ... 14 <u>The LORD shall fight for you</u>, and ye shall hold your peace.**

If Israel remains meek, then it demonstrates their

faith in their Messiah, the Son of God. Isaiah 29:19-20:

> 19 The meek also <u>shall increase their joy</u> in the LORD, and the poor among men shall <u>rejoice in the Holy One of Israel</u>.
>
> 20 <u>For the terrible one is brought to nought</u> [nothing], <u>and the scorner is consumed, and all that watch for iniquity are cut off</u> . . .

20

Revelation 20

Once an offender is captured, there is the arrest and the need for a place of incarceration. An angel is dispatched from heaven who has the keys for the dungeon and a chain to bind the criminal. Revelation 20:1-3:

> 1 **And I saw an angel come down from heaven, having the key of the bottomless pit and a great chain in his hand.** 2 **And he laid hold on the dragon, that old serpent, which is the Devil, and Satan, and bound him a thousand years,** 3 **And cast him into the bottomless pit, and shut him up, and set a seal upon him, that he should deceive the nations no more, till the thousand years should be fulfilled: and after that he must be loosed a little season.**

We are told that Satan will be bound for one thousand years after which he will be "loosed" for a season. This is not a test of Satan's rehabilitation, but a test for those who then live upon the earth. We will see shortly.

There are the twenty-four elders who sit upon seats of judgment along with God the Father and God the Son. Those witnesses for the Gospel of the Kingdom which were martyred by decapitation will also live and reign with the "KING OF KINGS, AND LORD OF LORDS" (Rev. 19:16). Verse 4:

> 4 **And I saw thrones, and they sat upon them, and judgment was given unto them: and I saw the souls of them that were beheaded for the witness of Jesus, and for the word of God, and which had not worshipped the beast, neither his image, neither had received his mark upon their foreheads, or in their hands; and they lived and reigned with Christ a thousand years.**

There will be two resurrections from the dead. The second one will be subject to "the second death." Let us look at it this way. Christ's death on the Cross is sufficient to save everyone who ever lived. He died for all. Eventually, all shall be resurrected from the dead. Here are Jesus' words. John 5:25-29:

> **25 Verily, verily, I say unto you, <u>The hour is coming, and now is, when the dead shall hear the voice of the Son of God: and they that hear shall live</u>. 26 For as the Father hath life in himself; so hath he given to the Son to have life in himself; 27 And hath given him authority to execute judgment also, because he is the Son of man. 28 Marvel not at this: for the hour is coming, <u>in the which all that are in the graves shall hear his voice, 29 And shall come forth; they that have done good, unto the resurrection of life; and they that have done evil, unto the resurrection of damnation.</u>**

In our present text, John is talking about the first resurrection from the dead. Of course, those who endure the Tribulation will still be upon the earth as well as some Gentiles who chose to bless the children of Abraham. The second resurrection from the dead will occur after the one thousand year reign of Christ. Revelation 20:5-6:

> **5 But the rest of the dead lived not again until the thousand years were finished. This is the first resurrection. 6 Blessed**

and holy is he that hath part in the first resurrection: on such the second death hath no power, but they shall be priests of God and of Christ, and shall reign with him a thousand years.

One thousand years after Christ begins ruling from Jerusalem as King, certain events will occur. Satan will be released from incarceration. He has not changed. Satan and those who will follow him in the rebellion will receive God's quick and effective response. Verses 7-10:

7 And when the thousand years are expired, Satan shall be loosed out of his prison, 8 And shall go out to deceive the nations which are in the four quarters of the earth, Gog and Magog, to gather them together to battle: the number of whom is as the sand of the sea. 9 And they went up on the breadth of the earth, and compassed the camp of the saints about, and the beloved city: and fire came down from God out of heaven, and devoured them. 10 And the devil that deceived them was cast into the lake of fire and brimstone, where the beast and the false prophet are, and shall be tormented day and night for

ever and ever.

In addition to the temporary release and rebellion of Satan, the second resurrection will occur. Each will stand before God and the books revealing their deeds will be opened. This is call the Great White Throne Judgment and all those who are subject to the second resurrection will be "judged every man according to their works." Verses 11-13:

> 11 **And I saw a great white throne, and him that sat on it, from whose face the earth and the heaven fled away; and there was found no place for them.** 12 **And I saw the dead, small and great, stand before God; and the books were opened: and another book was opened, which is the book of life: and the dead were judged out of those things which were written in the books, according to their works.** 13 **And the sea gave up the dead which were in it; and death and hell delivered up the dead which were in them: <u>and they were judged every man according to their works</u>.**

What will be the eternal punishment? It is called the Lake of Fire. Jesus continually warned those He taught about this place of torment. He describes it as a place where the worm never dies and having an unquenchable fire. Verses 14-15:

> 14 And death and hell were cast into the lake of fire. This is the second death. 15 And whosoever was not found written in the book of life was cast into the lake of fire.

21

Revelation 21

Let us call the last two or three chapters of Revelation "the ultimate conclusion." God is bringing His restoration of Creation, including the redemption of man, to its grand finale. John is a witness to this through his vision. The great battle of Armageddon is behind us, the King is victorious, and His people, true Israel, are safe. In Daniel's prophecy, there were five things that God foretold He would complete. Let us keep an eye out for them. If they have not been completed to this point, then they will be. How do we know this? God is faithful to the Word of God. Daniel 9:24:

> 24 **Seventy weeks are determined** upon thy people and upon thy holy city, [1] to finish the transgression, and [2] to make an end of sins, and [3] to make reconciliation for iniquity, and [4] to bring in

everlasting righteousness, and [5 to seal up the vision and prophecy, and [6] to anoint the most Holy.

I have been asked why there are only six and not seven. I thought about it. I believe that the answer is that God completed Creation in six days and rested on the seventh. Think of it as the Eternal Sabbath. Also, the number seven is often used for perfection.

With that said, let us find out what John sees now. Revelation 21:1-1:

1 And <u>I saw a new heaven and a new earth</u>: for the first heaven and the first earth were passed away; and there was no more sea.

Imagine waking up and looking about you to find that everything is new. From John's observation, we can surmise that he is now on the restored earth and looking upwards towards heaven. Below, the word *tabernacle* signifies that the dwelling place of God and the presence of God will be among His people. Verses 3-4:

2 And I John saw the holy city, new Jerusalem, coming down from God out of heaven, prepared as a bride adorned for

her husband. 3 And I heard a great voice out of heaven saying, Behold, the tabernacle of God is with men, and he will dwell with them, and they shall be his people, and God himself shall be with them, and be their God.

The past seven years were the greatest of tribulations that the world has ever seen. Like the Flood, when it was over, it was a new world. There will be no more tears or crying because what was in the past is now gone. Verse 4:

4 And God shall wipe away all tears from their eyes; and there shall be no more death, neither sorrow, nor crying, neither shall there be any more pain: for the former things are passed away.

Notice in the following verses that it is the Lord Jesus Christ Who is speaking from the throne. Jesus declares that He is the Alpha and Omega. These are respectively the first and last letter of the Greek alphabet. He is signifying that He is the Beginning and the End. Verses 5-6:

5 And he that sat upon the throne said, Behold, I make all things new. And he said unto me, Write: for these words are

true and faithful. 6 And he said unto me, It is done. I am Alpha and Omega, the beginning and the end. I will give unto him that is athirst of the fountain of the water of life freely. 7 He that overcometh shall inherit all things; and I will be his God, and he shall be my son.

Verse 7 speaks about those who have overcome while the following verse speaks about those who will be judged and punished. Verse 8:

8 But the fearful, and unbelieving, and the abominable, and murderers, and whoremongers, and sorcerers, and idolaters, and all liars, shall have their part in the lake which burneth with fire and brimstone: which is the second death.

An angel appeared to John to take him to another place and reveal to him something glorious. They went to a vantage point which was high atop a mountain so that he could fully behold the sight. Verses 9-10:

9 And there came unto me one of the seven angels which had the seven vials full of the seven last plagues, and talked with me, saying, Come hither, I

will shew thee the bride, the Lamb's wife. 10 **And he carried me away in the spirit to a great and high mountain, and shewed me that great city, the holy Jerusalem, descending out of heaven from God,**

We discover that the Lamb's wife is the new Jerusalem. John begins to describe what he sees in his own words. Verses 11-13:

11 **Having the glory of God: and her light was like unto a stone most precious, even like a jasper stone, clear as crystal;** 12 **And had a wall great and high, and had twelve gates, and at the gates twelve angels, and names written thereon, which are the names of the twelve tribes of the children of Israel:** 13 **On the east three gates; on the north three gates; on the south three gates; and on the west three gates.**

How can this not be about Israel? Did you notice that the names of the twelve tribes of Israel are memorialized on the twelve gates? Furthermore, there are twelve foundations. Each with the name of the twelve Kingdom Apostles who were His disciples while He was on earth. These men remained with

Him during His three year ministry. The twelve included Judas' replacement named Matthias who, by lot, "was numbered with the eleven apostles" (Acts 1:26). These twelve continued to preach the Gospel of the Kingdom after His Ascension. Verse 14:

> 14 **And the wall of the city had twelve foundations, and in them the names of the twelve apostles of the Lamb.**

For the Apostle John to mentally grasp the immensity of its size, the angel measures it for him. In the following, it is important to know that a *furlong* is an imperial measurement that is equal to *six hundred sixty feet*. Verses 15-16:

> 15 **And he [the angel] that talked with me had a golden reed to measure the city, and the gates thereof, and the wall thereof. 16 And the city lieth foursquare, and the length is as large as the breadth: and he measured the city with the reed, twelve thousand furlongs. The length and the breadth and the height of it are equal.**

Using simple mathematics, I multiplied twelve thousand furlongs by six hundred and sixty feet. The sum being in feet, I divided it by the amount in the common mile which is five thousand two hundred and eighty feet per mile. The quotient is exactly one thousand five hundred miles. This is the same measurement for its length, width, and height. These measurements, being the same, make it a cube. Imagine John watching as this new Jerusalem descends from heaven.

The angel continues with more measurements. Verse 17:

> 17 **And he measured the wall thereof, an hundred and forty and four cubits, according to the measure of a man, that is, of the angel.**

A cubit is a measurement taken from the anatomy of a man. It is the length between the elbow and the wrist. It varies between eighteen and twenty-two inches. If we use twenty inches, then the one hundred forty-four cubits yield the width of the wall to be two hundred forty feet. John describes some of the materials used. The City must have been a dazzling sight to see! Verses 18-21:

> 18 **And the building of the wall of it was of jasper: and the city was pure gold, like unto clear glass. 19 And the foundations of the wall of the city were gar-**

nished with all manner of precious stones. The first foundation was jasper; the second, sapphire; the third, a chalcedony; the fourth, an emerald; 20 The fifth, sardonyx; the sixth, sardius; the seventh, chrysolite; the eighth, beryl; the ninth, a topaz; the tenth, a chrysoprasus; the eleventh, a jacinth; the twelfth, an amethyst. 21 And the twelve gates were twelve pearls; every several [individual] gate was of one pearl: and the street of the city was pure gold, as it were transparent glass.

Everyone who knows ancient Jerusalem will look for the Temple. John was no different because the Temple was the focal point. John quickly notices that there is no temple in the new Jerusalem. Verses 22-23:

22 And I saw no temple therein: for the Lord God Almighty and the Lamb are the temple of it. 23 And the city had no need of the sun, neither of the moon, to shine in it: for the glory of God did lighten it, and the Lamb is the light thereof.

Can you imagine there being no sun or moon? It does

not say that they no longer exist. It says that there is no need for them. Why? It is because God and the Lamb will be the light.

As John continues, keep in mind that "the nations" are the Gentiles. They are the non-Jews. So, the nations still exist after the great battle. Those called "the kings of the earth" are rulers over the Gentile nations. Verse 24:

> **24 And the nations of them which are saved shall walk in the light of it: and the kings of the earth do bring their glory and honour into it.**

Can you imagine leaving the gates of a city open all the time? What is there to worry about if God Himself is providing the security? Verse 25:

> **25 And the gates of it shall not be shut at all by day: for there shall be no night there.**

There is no night. So, the gates remain open. Each of "the kings of the earth" will come to Jerusalem to bring "glory and honour" to the King of Kings. Verse 26:

> **26 And they shall bring the glory and**

honour of the nations into it.

However, we see below that only those whose names are written in the Lamb's book of life may enter. How then are these kings to bring their "glory and honor" to the King. Consider this prophecy. Zechariah 8:23:

> 23 **Thus saith the LORD of hosts; In those days it shall come to pass, that ten men shall take hold out of all languages of the nations, even shall take hold of the skirt of him that is a Jew, saying, <u>We will go with you: for we have heard that God is with you.</u>**

When the Kingdom is established in the new Jerusalem, the Jews will be honored with the role of priests to the Almighty God. The true and faithful were chosen for this purpose since the days of Moses. Exodus 19:6:

> 6 **And <u>ye shall be unto me a kingdom of priests, and an holy nation</u>. These are the words which thou shalt speak unto the children of Israel.**

It concludes with Revelation 21:27:

> 27 **And there shall in no wise [way] enter**

into it any thing that defileth, neither whatsoever worketh abomination, or maketh a lie: but they which are written in the Lamb's book of life.

22

Revelation 22

This is the final chapter of Revelation which completes the Bible. We are given a vision of restored Creation with the Kingdom established. The vision is wonderful and glorious with life flowing from "the throne of God." Revelation 22:1:

> 1 **And he shewed me a pure river of water of life, clear as crystal, proceeding out of the throne of God and of the Lamb.**

We find that "the tree of life" which was originally in Eden is now growing in Jerusalem. It bears its fruit continually. Verse 2:

> 2 **In the midst of the street of it, and on either side of the river, was there the tree of life, which bare twelve manner**

**of fruits, and yielded her fruit every
month: and the leaves of the tree were
for the healing of the nations.**

In Genesis 3, as the result of Satan's temptation
and the fall of Adam and Eve, God cursed the individuals involved and their offspring. He also cursed
Creation. Now, this curse has been removed. Verses
3-4:

**3 And there shall be no more curse: but
the throne of God and of the Lamb shall
be in it; and his servants shall serve
him: 4 And they shall see his face; and
his name shall be in their foreheads.**

We are told again that the darkness is gone. God and
the Lamb are the light and their reign will be forever.
Verse 5:

**5 And there shall be no night there; and
they need no candle, neither light of the
sun; for the Lord God giveth them light:
and they shall reign for ever and ever.**

The angel who was showing all this to John
states that what John has seen is trustworthy and
true. Verse 6:

6 And he said unto me, These sayings are faithful and true: and the Lord God of the holy prophets sent his angel to shew unto his servants the things which must shortly be done.

As the book of Revelation draws to a close, the Lord Jesus Christ speaks to John about His return saying, "I come quickly." Those who choose to believe the Word of God by having faith in these sayings will be blessed. Verse 7:

7 Behold, I come quickly: blessed is he that keepeth the sayings of the prophecy of this book.

We can only imagine the impact all of this had upon the Apostle John. These visions affected both his mind and his emotions. Being overwhelmed, He falls before the angel who tells him not to do this. Verses 8-9:

8 And I John saw these things, and heard them. And when I had heard and seen, I fell down to worship before the feet of the angel which shewed me these things. **9** Then saith he unto me, See thou do it not: for I am thy fellowservant, and of thy brethren the proph-

**ets, and of them which keep the sayings
of this book: worship God.**

John is given instruction concerning the information
he received. Unlike Daniel who was told to seal up
information, John is told this prophecy pertains to
the present. However, its purpose is to inform and
not the change anyone. The four gospels were sent to
change the hearts of men. This book outlines the future and it is intended to strengthen the conviction of
the Kingdom Believers. Verses 10-11:

> 10 **And he saith unto me, Seal not the
> sayings of the prophecy of this book:
> for the time is at hand. 11 He that is un-
> just, let him be unjust still: and he
> which is filthy, let him be filthy still:
> and he that is righteous, let him be
> righteous still: and he that is holy, let
> him be holy still.**

A statement in made by the Lord Jesus Christ
to those who will receive this book of prophecy. His
return is imminent and He alone is worthy to judge
the living and the dead. To some He will give a reward and to others judgment. Verses 12-13:

> 12 **And, behold, I come quickly; and my
> reward is with me, to give every man**

according as his work shall be. 13 I am Alpha and Omega, the beginning and the end, the first and the last.

It is clear from the following that He is speaking to those who are saved by the Gospel of the Kingdom. For those believers, the Law and commandments are still active. Nothing had changed. Jesus stated, "Think not that I am come to destroy the law, or the prophets: I am not come to destroy, but to fulfil" (Matt. 5:17). For the faithful who endure until the end, they will live in the Kingdom. Verses 14-15:

14 Blessed are they that do his commandments, that they may have right to the tree of life, and may enter in through the gates into the city. 15 For without are dogs, and sorcerers, and whoremongers, and murderers, and idolaters, and whosoever loveth and maketh a lie.

The information which John received is to be sent to the seven churches. These a representative of all the Kingdom Churches. Jesus Christ is the Son of David and rightful heir to David's throne. Verse 16:

16 I Jesus have sent mine angel to testify unto you these things in the churches. I

**am the root and the offspring of David,
and the bright and morning star.**

An invitation is made by the Spirit and the Bride to come and join them. To whom is this invitation made? It is made to the children of Abraham. This is part of the reward for those who remain faithful until the end. Verse 17:

17 **And the Spirit and the bride say, Come. And let him that heareth say, Come. And let him that is athirst come. And whosoever will, let him take the water of life freely.**

In the following verses, there is a warning to all those who would alter the Word of God. The Spirit alone is entrusted with the inspiration of Scripture. Verses 18-19:

18 **For I testify unto every man that heareth the words of the prophecy of this book, [1] If any man shall add unto these things, God shall add unto him the plagues that are written in this book: 19 And [2] if any man shall take away from the words of the book of this prophecy, God shall take away his part out of the book of life, and out of the**

holy city, and from the things which are written in this book.

Few take this seriously because people add, change, and delete God's Word all the time. The Serpent in the Garden of Eden was the first to alter what God said to Adam and Eve. How did that work out for him? And, because they believed Satan, how did that work out for them? We should heed this warning.

Jesus Christ Who is truth and also the Word of God testifies to all that is disclosed in this book. He assures the readers that His return will surely happen and, when it does, it will happen quickly. Verse 20:

20 He which testifieth these things saith, Surely I come quickly. Amen. Even so, come, Lord Jesus.

Revelation closes with a blessing. The grace of Jesus Christ Who is the Messiah and the Son of God is Israel's Passover Lamb. He died for them and is with them always even unto the end. Verse 21:

21 The grace of our Lord Jesus Christ be with you all. Amen.

Epilogue

The book of Revelation is considered frightening to some. I can remember, as a child, my mother said she did not want to read Revelation. When I asked her why, she told me that she was afraid. To those of you who have similar feelings about Revelation, I will tell you this. The opposite of fear is faith. Faith is not based upon our feelings. It is based upon believing and trusting the Word of God.

Many people tell me that they believe. They have faith! They go to religious services every week. Oh yes, they also contribute generously. They volunteer at such-and-such. They quote bits and pieces from the Bible, but really do not understand it as a whole. As a teacher of the Bible, I will tell you that the majority of both Christians and Jews believe what they have been taught. They trust the person who taught them. So, there is no need to read God's Word. What is the difference?

I talk to pastors and when they find out that I

write commentaries, they scoff at me. "Oh. We don't like commentaries. We only read the Bible." So, you only read the Bible in church. "Yes!" You do not explain what it means. "Of course I tell them what it means." That, my friend, is commentary. Now, preachers and teachers may be inspired as they teach, but their "commentary" or explanations are not authoritative or equal to the Word of God.

Commentary must be seen for what it is. It is someone who is explaining God's Word, teaching God's Word, and applying God's Word. How then should the hearers or readers react? Paul gives the perfect example. A group of people came to hear him and they listened with an open mind, but they fact-checked. These were the Bereans mentioned in Acts. Luke wrote, "These were more noble than those in Thessalonica, in that they received the word with all readiness of mind, and searched the scriptures daily, whether those things were so" (Acts 17:11). God closed His revelation to mankind with a warning that carried with it a curse. Yet, they rationalized away the warning as if it does not apply to them. Revelation 22:18-19

> 18 . . . **If any man shall add unto these things, God shall add unto him the plagues that are written in this book: 19 And if any man shall take away from**

the words of the book of this prophecy, God shall take away his part out of the book of life, and out of the holy city, and from the things which are written in this book

Every believer must put Scripture above everything and everyone else. The Word of God must always take precedence. Why is this not done?

I like to use the statement, "People know what they know because that is what they were taught to know." They confuse knowledge and understanding with memorization. Learning is not hearing, memorizing, and regurgitating. That is indoctrination. Most of those who are taught in seminaries and theological schools are indoctrinated. They are to memorize the accepted facts from their sect or denomination. They study the history of the church and the great thoughts of the men of God like Augustine, Calvin, Luther, Darby, and others. Many pastors can quote these men with authority. However, at best, they are nothing more than brilliant opinions of men. I tell my students and readers that commentaries, including my own, are opinions to be considered, but Scripture is the final authority.

This problem will prove to be eternally fatal for a large majority of "religious" people. They choose to follow customs, traditions, and the vain philosophies or teachings of men. It happened with the Pharisees during Jesus' time. It is no different now. The Word of God was present with them in the flesh, but they would not listen. Now, we have the written Word of God in our hands, but they will not read it. How sad. All the begging and pleading will not move them. As a result, by their own free will, they will face the ultimate consequence of rejecting the Word of God as detailed in Revelation.

Everything is about God. He is the Creator, Sustainer, and the One Who rewards or punishes. The only way that we can truly know Him is through His Word. May God bless you with the joy that comes from having faith in His Word.

Respectfully,
Dr. David Alan Greene

Other GraceWord
Publications

Complete Surveys Of The Bible:

Letters To Theophilus
The Glorious Destiny Of Israel
The Hidden Gospel: Once Hidden But Now Reveal.

Expositional Commentaries Of The Bible:

1st Corinthians: Dispensationally Considered
1st & 2nd Thessalonians: Disp. Considered
1st & 2nd Timothy & Titus: Disp. Considered
2nd Corinthians: Dispensationally Considered
Acts: Dispensationally Considered
Colossians & Philemon: Disp. Considered
Ephesians: Dispensationally Considered
Galatians: Dispensationally Considered
Hebrews: Dispensationally Considered
Philippians: Dispensationally Considered
Romans: Dispensationally Considered

The Gospel of John: Dispensationally Considered
The Gospel of Luke: Dispensationally Considered
The Gospel of Mark: Dispensationally Considered
The Gospel of Matthew: Disp. Considered
The Seven Hebrew Epistles: Disp. Considered

Other Books

How Am I Wired?
Two Distinct Gospel Messages Of The N.T.

About The Author

Dr. David Alan Greene has over thirty-five years of experience as an insurance agent selling both property and casualty as well as life insurance. During his career, he taught and explained the content and meaning of policies to his clients. Now retired, he devotes much of his time to teaching the Bible.

He obtained his Bachelor of Theology, Master of Biblical Studies, and Ph.D. in Biblical Studies from Evangelical Theological Seminary where he holds the position of Dean of Graduate Studies. He also holds a Ph.D. in Christian Counseling. He has written numerous biblical commentaries and books on rightly dividing the Word of Truth.